WHAT THEY'RE SAYING ...

"I'd thought a wilderness experience was no longer possible in New Hampshire, until Kim Nilsen opened up the vast, sparsely populated North Country with the new Cohos Trail, a route for experienced backcountry travelers who want real mountain solitude.

And Kim's anecdotes about this storied region—which he knows better than many of us know our own backyards—make this book as entertaining as it is informative."

~Michael Lanza, outdoor writer, and author of *The Ultimate Guidebook to Backcountry Travel*

"This book and the trail it covers, continue the tradition of high quality work I have come to expect from the people who work on New Hampshire trails.

The trail itself is an interesting exploration of the forest that makes up the Great North Woods."

~Bob Spoerl, NH Division of Parks and Recreation

"Too many trail guides are scant in detail or just plain boring. *The Cohos Trail Guide* is neither. In describing this great new footpath and the wonderful country it traverses, Kim brings to novice and expert alike a keen sense of the North Country's rich history and outdoor legacy.

If you read this book, you'll have no choice but to put on a pack and go!"

~John Harrigan of Colebrook, newspaper publisher, *NH Sunday News* columnist, outdoor writer, and veteran hiker

"Trek along with writer Kim Nilsen through northern New Hampshire as you've never seen it before, along the newly developed Cohos Trail.

It's an adventure replete with old logging trails, lost backcountry paths, forgotten ridge runs—all linked together to accord the best the North Country has to offer.

For trailblazer Nilsen, the creation of the Cohos Trail is the fullfillment of a 20-year dream. For his readers, it's a treat right out of the guidebooks of the past. He weaves lore of the north with up-close encounters with such natural treasures as Baldhead and Mt. Muise, Kelsey Notch, Huntington Cascade, Sanguinary Mountain, and scores of other fabled places.

Kim Nilsen has put together a book which will be welcomed by anyone who dreams of leaving the well-traveled byways in search of places where the true North Country can still be found in its original state."

~Charles J. Jordan, Editor, *Northern New Hampshire Magazine*

THE
COHOS TRAIL

THE GUIDEBOOK TO
NEW HAMPSHIRE'S
GREAT UNKNOWN

THE COHOS TRAIL

THE GUIDEBOOK TO
NEW HAMPSHIRE'S
GREAT UNKNOWN

Kim Robert Nilsen

NICOLIN FIELDS
PUBLISHING
INCORPORATED
North Hampton, NH 03862

Published by Nicolin Fields Publishing, Inc.
3 Red Fox Road, North Hampton, NH 03862
NicolinFields.com

Printed in Canada.

Cover design by Kim Robert Nilsen
USGS maps modified by Kim Robert Nilsen
Photos by Kim Robert Nilsen or as noted
Book interior design and layout by Linda Chestney

Library of Congress Cataloging-in-Publication Data

Nilsen, Kim Robert, 1948-
    The Cohos Trail : the guidebook to New Hampshire's great unknown / by Kim Robert Nilsen ; [edited by Linda Chestney ; maps by Kim Robert Nilsen ; photos by Kim Robert Nilsen or as noted].
        p. cm.
    Includes index.
    ISBN 0-9637077-7-9 (pbk.)
    1. Hiking--New Hampshire--Cohos Trail--Guidebooks. 2. Cohos Trail (N.H.)--Guidebooks. I. Title: Guidebook to New Hampshire's great Unknown. II. Chestney, Linda, 1952- III. Title.

GV199.42.N42 C655 2000

                                                                00-02585

Dedication

To the great women in my life—
my wife, Catherine,
my daughter, Shyloah,
my daughter, Willow,
my granddaughter,
Sage Elizabeth.

Contents

Acknowledgements

Projects the scale of The Cohos Trail (CT) can't be accomplished alone. Scores of people have been involved, and most have been greatly supportive of the effort. I just have to say thank you in the most sincere terms that I know how. After all, it hasn't been much more than three years since the first public meeting was called in Lancaster, New Hampshire about the possible development of The Cohos Trail. And now—in that short period of time—we are on the verge of opening one of the great long trails in the Northeast. I am humbled by the help I've received.

Firstly, a special thank you to people in various positions within New Hampshire state government. Robert Spoerl, at the Trails Bureau in Concord, could not have been more helpful and more spirited in his support. I am indebted to Bob and appreciative of his level and fair manner, his thoroughness, and his understanding of the dynamics that exist between trail builders and land owners.

Thomas Miner of NH Forests and Lands was extremely helpful and made several terrific suggestions that resulted in a better trail system. Also thank you to James Carter at Land Management who orchestrated the land-use contract. Bob McGregor of Forest and Lands at the Lancaster office helped me (and volunteers) gain access to lands and information. Brad Presby of the Trails Bureau (Lancaster office) also saved me from a fate far worse than death in the backcountry—but that's another story. Johanna Lyons went to bat for us for trail grant funding.

These State employees have been so supportive of the effort that I am now a certified fan of state government. Imagine that!

Thank you to David Dernbach of North Country Trailmaster. No one has gotten behind The Cohos Trail project like David. He is the pit bull of the CT. He takes everyone by the scruff of the neck and shakes him or her a bit so that they see the potential of this long footpath in the Coos woods. He is the greatest. And thank you to his many young trailmasters who worked on the path during the summer of 1998 and 1999. Also kudos to former trailmaster and trail builder extraordinaire, Tracy Rexford (T-Rex) of Lancaster.

And what does one say about Steve Barba, managing partner of The Balsams Grand Resort Hotel in Dixville Notch? To say that Steve is a big booster of The Cohos Trail simply isn't saying enough. Steve is the best sounding board there is and an inexhaustible resource of ideas and local history. The man is amazing.

To the news media—I'm grateful to *Coos County Democrat* managing editor Gene Ehlert and his wife, Linda,—they always gave me a couch to crash on. And Gene tramped more woods with me than I suspect he ever wanted to. And I'm most appreciative of Edith Tucker, the *Democrat's* ace reporter who has covered the story so well and who has given me great advise along the way. Also, I'm delighted that Charlie Jordan wanted to feature the trail in his *Northern New Hampshire Magazine.* And thanks to John Harrigan, publisher of the *Colebrook News and Sentinel* and *The Democrat,* who knows the north so well he can describe every backwater stream and rock knob.

Thanks to John Lane of Lancaster, who knows Nash Stream Forest well, and who let me "live" at his Silver Brook camp while working on the trail. And thanks Dan Tucker, Edith's husband, who takes care of the threadbare books for the little association we run.

To the trail builders—Jack Pepau and his sons, Chad and Chris, of Stark for their great effort; Wayne and Joyce Liptak of Campton, the very best husband and wife team in the north; Nate Richards and family of Colebrook, who laid out the new Sanguinary Summit Trail on the CT; Doug Mayer of the Randolph Mountain Club, who has kept me informed of the terrific work that the RMC has done on Owlshead and Starr King; Mary Ellen Cannon of Lancaster and George Glidden of Whitefield for their work on the Headwaters Road and Gadwah Notch; and to the two super loggers from Crown Vantage Corp. whose expert skill with chain saws made it possible for the trail to advance much faster than was originally planned. The cutters were arranged by Haven Neal, an independent forester and expert on the logging and paper industries. Without his help, the trail would still be rough and tough to follow.

To the landowners—A warm thank you to Fred Foss of Columbia, for the okay to put the trail up on Baldhead South; to Malcolm Washburn of Colebrook for permitting a link over his holding between Mead lands and Mr. Foss's parcel; to Don Merski of Mead Paper Company, whose sensible land-use and logging practices have improved recreational opportunities and wildlife habitat on the company's vast holdings while supplying valuable forest products that we all use everyday; to the State of New Hampshire for allowing access and new trail work in the Nash Stream Forest and other parcels of State land; to George Pozzuto of the USFS Androscoggin Ranger District and to the United States Forest Service who manage the great jewel of our public woodlands, The White Mountain National Forest.

And last but not least, a warm thank you to the Tillotson Corporation of Dixville Notch, which has permitted new trail and links over 13,000 acres of high ground on the corporation's lands. Thanks to International Paper Company for supplying maps of their land holdings in the north, which helped us lay out the trail accurately and not trespass on the lands of others. To Champion International Corporation's Allan Peterson and Donald Tase for information and policies about Champion holdings and their voicing legitimate concerns about hikers and campers in the northern working forests; to US Generation of New England for enlightening us to the easements the power company maintains in the Connecticut Lakes region and the verbal support for creating some new trail in that area.

I must thank David Govatski of the USFS and the manager of the Audubon's Pondicherry Wildlife Reserve. David is an absolute fountain of information about the national forest and about old or abandoned trails and logging tracts.

Penny Clark of Dunbarton has slaved away on the huge Cohos Trail Association website, www.cohostrail.org. It's a gem and she is the reason for it. Thank you very much, Penny.

To the selectmen of the Town of Stark, NH who are considering donating some land at the old Stark dump to the association so that we might build a taxable structure on the land to help in some small way channel dollars into Stark's town budget. Special thanks to educators, like Andy Coppinger, former principal of Stratford High School, who put students to work on the trail and who has organized the school's special trail projects in Nash Stream Forest.

To Diana Pelletier who channeled Americorps volunteers our way to work on the system.

I'm appreciative of the interest of Mike Lanza, senior writer for *Backpacker* magazine (December 1999 issue), and to Linda Chestney of Nicolin Fields Publishing, Inc., who had faith in me and the project, and who agreed to publish this guidebook.

Thanks to the folks at Hiker's Paradise in Gorham, the hiker's hostel. Thanks Bruce Pettingill for the inexpensive digs, great breakfast, and good company.

And kudos to Bob and Mary Julian of New Mexico, whose book, *Place Names of the White Mountains*, yielded valuable information about the origins of the many monikers of the north. I could not resist using their term "Oh Be Joyful" in place of alcohol when writing about Mt. Eisenhower.

And I couldn't do this mammoth task without the support of my wife, Catherine, my two daughters, Shyloah and Willow, and my granddaughter, Sage Elizabeth, who has already been to the summit of North Percy while riding on my back. And thanks to Bob Merz, my wife's dad, who has let me stay at his home in the White Mountains while working on the trail.

It has been the utmost pleasure working with all the folks listed above. And it has been inspiring to see people work so hard on the idea that wonderful Coos County, New Hampshire ought to have a world-class, long-distance hiking trail, so that people may discover just how remarkable a place this remote and grand county really is.

With gratitude,
Kim Robert Nilsen

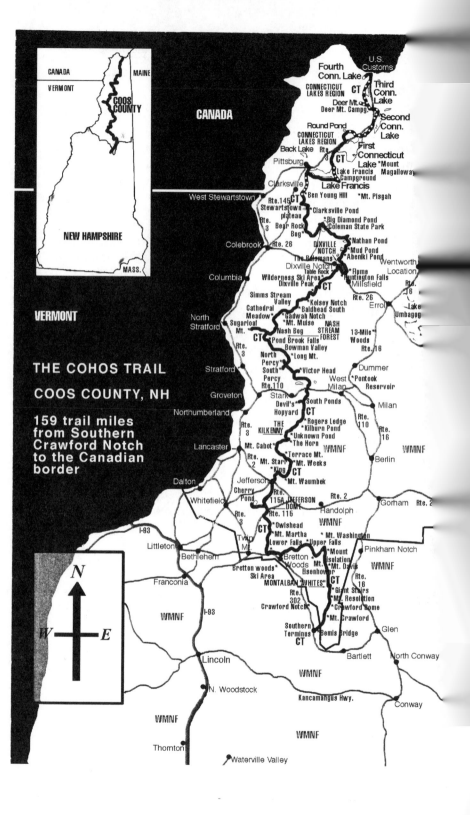

THE COHOS TRAIL

COOS COUNTY, NH

159 trail miles from Southern Crawford Notch to the Canadian border

Introduction

The Inside Scoop ...

At this writing, The Cohos Trail (CT) is still being developed. By the summer of 2000, you will be able to hike more than 115 miles of formally open trail system from a few miles northwest of the New Hampshire community of Bartlett, to the lofty hill and lake country of Stewartstown, New Hampshire.

You may trek all the way from Notchland in southern Crawford Notch to Jefferson village on existing White Mountain National Forest, Appalachian Mountain Club, and Randolph Mountain Club trails. From there you may venture north into the remote mountainous country of the Kilkenny, the Nash Stream Forest, and the Dixville Notch region, backcountry areas that few people have ever hiked.

The trail north of Stewartstown is in the planning stages at this time. There is no formal trail system as yet from Coleman State Park to the Canadian border. This guide sketches out some route alternatives northward, particularly along existing old farm lanes and little used public ways.

But The Cohos Trail Association, which authorizes this guide, does not advocate hiking in woodlands in remote far northern regions now, unless you obtain permission to do so from Champion International Corporation and other property owners in the region. And you must obey rather strict rules of land use, as virtually all land owners in the far north permit day use only. People apprehended for camping out and/or building cooking fires on private lands face prosecution and severe fines from local justices.

CஐCஐCஐ

Prologue

I first proposed the creation of The Cohos Trail in 1978 in an editorial in the *Coos* (pronounced coe-ahhs) *County Democrat* newspaper published at Lancaster, New Hampshire. I was a reporter for the little weekly paper then, and I lived with my family in a home we built from scratch in a field in the threadbare, but beautiful, Great North Woods town of Dalton. My wife and I, and our two very young daughters, hiked in the backcountry often. I got to know first hand most of the remote country sketched out in this guide.

When snowmobiling became a large winter recreational sport in the 1960s and '70s, I was impressed by the ability of various new snowmobile clubs to create trail systems in remote country. Why, I thought, couldn't hikers, cross-country skiers, bicyclists, and back woods buffs, put a trail together like the snowmobilers had done in a short period of time?

In 1996, while I was sitting with topographical maps of the country north of the White Mountains in my lap, looking for a bushwhacking route northeast from the summit of Sugarloaf Mountain in the Nash Stream State Forest, I realized that what I was looking at was a potential route that could link stretches of existing trail, and old logging and skid roads, together to form a long-distance trail like the one I proposed so long ago. This path could be strung together through much of Coos County—the whole length of it, I thought. I did a bit of research, re-hiked some trails and little-traveled woodlands I hadn't seen in quite a few years, and wrote a very brief proposal for the New Hampshire Department of Resources and Economic Development to look over.

With the help of folks (see acknowledgments) from the state, federal agencies, from paper and timber companies, from hiking and snowmobiling club members, from North Country educators and their students, from local outdoors enthusiasts, and from the region's media, The Cohos Trail became a reality.

The Cohos Trail is soon to be New Hampshire's longest single through-trail system, winding eventually from southern Crawford Notch near the town of Bartlett, all the way to the Canadian border. Eventually you may also be able to continue the trek north into Quebec via trails being developed by the Sentiers Frontaliers hiking club of Lac Megantic, PQ.

WILDERNESS

Words
to Live By

The Bemis Bridge.
The first step on the Cohos Trail.

Snow Showers

Stories from the Back Woods

At 52 degrees below zero, strange things were happening. The mercury in the thermometer congealed in a ball at the very bottom of the instrument, and it wasn't budging. I didn't know if I should trust the reading or not... but nevertheless, the quicksilver stuck hard—at minus 52.

Real Men...

Only a fool goes outside in arctic cold this extreme. So I went outside. I took a bubble pipe (no, not the plastic soap bubble wand that kids use today, but a good, old-fashioned bubble pipe) with me.

Arctic cold is made of tempered steel. It has unimaginable strength. On this February night in 1969, in a back-of-yonder dubbed Coos County, New Hampshire, I walked into a steely wall. There was no moon, but the night was as bright as Broadway. Such a profusion of stars shown that the sky looked like dust caught in the footlights of the Great White Way. Jupiter, usually a wobbly, candle flame in the sky, was automobile-high-beam bright.

On such nights the air ceases to move, except to sink into abyssal pockets and become colder and colder as the night wears on. It was still as death, and quiet as deafness, except for an occasional "rifle shot" from the woods—a sap pocket expanding suddenly and bursting apart the overlying wood fibers of a tree.

I took the bubble pipe out, loaded the little thing with soap, and blew. Out came a stream of bubbles, clear and round for an instant, and then—magic—they turned the color of lake ice. They floated in front of me because there was no breath of wind to move them about. Then one of the little soap spheres landed on the porch. It shattered like glass.

Another landed and rolled—yes, rolled—down a porch plank. In New Hampshire's Great North Woods, well beyond the White Mountains, you can get away with things like this. No one is about to see me suffer bubble-pipe relapses, which I suppose, might have me committed to the state hospital at Concord some day.

There's Magic in Them Thar Woods

In Coos County—this huge forested realm in New Hampshire's far north—you enter a lost world. On the highway maps of the state, most of the territory up here is left blank. Cartographers simply don't know what to ink into their maps. It's the same thing that explorers like Henry Hudson, John Cabot, Ponce d'Leone, and Verazanno did when they sketched their first maps of the New World.

Maybe it's the utter cold that keeps people away. The county is home to only about 40,000 souls. The Cohos Trail, all 160 miles of it, passes through just two villages, and each has populations of fewer than 500. Maybe it's the distance from urban utopias that's the deciding factor. Everyone swarms about the White Mountains, but only a few hardy sapiens leak through Pinkham, Franconia, or Crawford Notches to make it into the lost world.

Or maybe it's this tongue-in-cheek craziness that holds the flatlanders at bay.

My Coos County madness didn't end with the bubble pipe incident. I go looking for this well-altered state of mind—brought on by being isolated in a million acres of woodland for too long— wherever I can find it.

How else do you explain a set of bagpipes on the summit of East Royce, and no hikers about, and no car at the trailhead parking spot? Or how about the big creosote post with the ski mask pulled over it and a cigar (placed in a drilled hole) sticking out of the mouth. And this in the middle of nowhere.

Then there were the five college students who lugged up to the summit of Jefferson a five-course meal, a table, chairs, wine hod, and a big, wooden hand-crank Victrola that had to have weighed 50 pounds. They removed their hiking gear, and were dressed in tuxes and flowing gowns. They sat down for a formal dinner, complete with crystal wine glasses and candelabra.

One day I got a call from a fellow in Columbia who said he had shot the biggest eastern coyote ever recorded in the state of New Hampshire. I went to photograph the poor creature for the little newspaper I worked for and found the guy had shot a German Shepherd stone-cold dead.

I almost forgot about the cracker who picked me up hitch hiking back to my car after canoeing the length of the Magalloway River. The passenger side floor of the old pickup truck he was driving was filled full with empty beer cans. He had cracked a fresh one and was nursing it along while we chatted. When he finished the beer, he tossed the can out the window with a well-practiced flick of the wrist. The can landed neatly in the bed of the truck, where it settled comfortably beside at least 200 other cans.

And There's More

And just recently, I was bushwhacking and marking new trail in an unknown pocket of woodlands between Mt. Muise and Baldhead, fully expecting to be alone all day. There are no trails and no prominent features to attract someone into this realm, and it takes many hours of walking in the backcountry just to get there. I climbed onto the flank of Baldhead, when I heard someone say, "Hey, I know you." I jumped. I turned to see a big, big man dressed in brown khakis striding toward me. It was Fred Foss, a gentleman who had designed computer systems for the Apollo moon missions. Tall, friendly, with a huge smile, Fred came over to shake my hand. "Say, aren't you that trail fella, Nilsen?" You'd never know he was in his late seventies.

Yes, the madness has extended to building The Cohos Trail, 160 trail miles of the damn thing over one-third of the length of the state. Strange things go on surrounding this venture, too.

Somebody left a handheld weed whacker high on Mt. Sanguinary. Odd. Why would someone leave a perfectly good tool like that up here? I leaned down, picked it up, and learned first hand why the tool was abandoned. A white-tailed hornet the size of a crow, from a huge nest just overhead, nailed me precisely between the eyes.

Got a call from a fellow who wants to offer his services to build hiker hostels near the trail. Good. His material of choice? Bales of straw.

A good friend of mine, a seasoned trail builder, too, was cutting blowdowns from the trail near Baldhead, when the beauty of the place got to him. He put his saw down and wandered about in the high mountain meadows to enjoy the country. He lost his way. Got "turned around," as we say. Now, he knows the woods and how to get out of them, so he bushwhacked downhill several miles to a road, then retraced his steps back to where he started. "You know," he said, "If one of my students had done what I did, I'd be all over him. No pack, no water, no compass. God!"

More Real Men

Went bushwhacking with State Biologist, Will Staats. Big mistake. He's a five-time gold-medal winner of the fir-forest Olympics. There is no man on the face of the earth who can move through blinding fir thicket at the hell-bent pace he sets. I found myself whimpering like a hungry puppy trying to follow him up the east side of North Percy Peak. Just when I thought I'd caught up to him, he'd call out from the hall of the mountain king and I'd realize I still had a thousand feet to go to scale the evergreen-needle prison walls.

Self-Reliance—and a Large Dose of Common Sense!

And so you see, in Coos County, above the Whites to the Canadian border, things get a bit skewed up here. Isolation breeds independence, self- reliance, and that special insanity known only to those from back of yonder.

So, after using my bubble pipe in the deep freeze, I came back in the house and decided to take a hot shower to warm up. In the bedroom off the bath, the window nearest the bathroom didn't have a storm window. So there was only one pane of glass separating the warm interior from 52 degrees below.

I took a long shower, one as hot as possible and filled the bath with steam. I got out and opened the door and toweled down. Steam rolled from the little water closet and filled the bedroom. As I threw a robe around myself, something caught my eye. Something moving. Something white. I went over to the window, below which was a big stuffed easy chair. The steam droplets cascading next to the window were turning white. Turning to snow. And the snow was falling onto the back of the stuffed chair and it was covered with a dusting of white. It was snowing *in* my bedroom. *Inside*!

So it must be the cold after all that keeps people away. I don't know why I stayed in this big lost corner of New Hampshire. Probably because I can blow bubblepipe bubbles at absolute zero and nobody up here pays me any mind. That, I like.

ෆෆෆ

Coos County
and The Cohos Trail

WHY THE COHOS TRAIL?

The Northeastern United States from Maine to Northern Virginia and Cleveland and Columbus, Ohio, supports nearly one-third of the entire population of the country. Eastern Canada, between Quebec City and the Toronto, London, Kitchner megalopolis, supports more than one-half of all of that nation's population. In short, nearly 100 million people reside in these rather compact areas, most about a long day's drive from the southern terminus of the Cohos Trail. All of us who live in this beehive put enormous pressure on the environment and its natural resources.

We are fortunate to have several pressure-relief valves in the Northeast. One is the long coastline from the mouth of the Potomac to Quoddy Head Light in eastern-most Maine. The other is a vast forested realm now often called The Northern Forest. This enormous carpet of woodlands encompasses most of the state of Maine, the northern half of New Hampshire, the Green Mountains of Vermont, and the Adirondacks and Catskills of New York state.

The Wilderness Experience

Tens of millions of people visit places within this great forest fastness each year. But few of us have the interest or skill to tackle this vast natural world on its own terms. But among the millions are those few souls who hunger for wilderness experiences and who possess skills enough to enjoy a true backcountry experience without sullying the natural environment.

For these people The Cohos Trail (CT) was created. It is a 160-mile-long trail system, along which an individual will be in remote country more than 90 percent of the time. To rely on oneself in such country for a week or longer, requires more than a little woods experience, a respect for the forces of nature, and a desire to experience nature first hand without the trappings of civilization.

A through-hike demands above-average skill, excellent physical condition, a very heavy and well-thought-out backpack, and the sense to leave the trail and its environs unspoiled, and any private property unmarred.

So the CT is decidedly not for everyone, although day-hiking, biking, or skiing in some of the system, is certainly manageable by many people (as is snowmobiling in those sections of the trail which can accommodate such craft).

Truly Rugged Wilderness

The trail does not boast a hut or lean-to system, at least not yet, so the hiker is exposed to the elements most of the time. If you are not skilled at staying outdoors a week at a time in inclement weather, then attempting The Cohos Trail is not the thing to do. The trail has been designed to be a rugged, no-nonsense wilderness experience—a real challenge—the likes of which the eastern U.S. doesn't offer much anymore. In some respects, it's odd that such a through trail in New Hampshire has never been put together, other than the famous Appalachian Trail.

Numerous states in the United States have such trails, including Vermont, the Granite State's nearest neighbor.

Before the idea for the trail was hatched, about 93 percent of the right of way existed in one form or another. About a third of the CT rides on the backs of existing hiking trails. Bits and pieces of logging roads and skid trails, railroad beds, backroads, state highway, snowmobile trail, moose paths and the like, are sprinkled throughout the huge county. So the CT existed for the most part, but it existed in limbo. It took a few new link trails to tie all the parts together into a distinct and challenging whole.

CBCBCB

FROM WHERE TO WHERE?

The Cohos Trail (CT) begins in the south at Notchland, five miles south of Crawford Notch State Park at the trailhead of the Davis Path. The Davis Path is a long and famous route up the southwest shoulder of the mountain mass that comprises Mount Washington. The trail ends in a remote saddle by the shores of a tiny fen surrounded by spruce and fir-clad hills. This little swamp pond is not far from where U.S. Route 3 terminates at the United States Customs House on the border with Quebec, Canada.

In between, the trail crosses the boundaries of a dozen towns and a few uninhabited, unincorporated places. If you look at a map of New Hampshire, you will see that Notchland lies to the west and north of the village of Bartlett, just north of a tight northward kink in the Saco River. It threads its way up and over the southern Presidential Range at Mt. Eisenhower more than 4,700 feet in elevation, and then descends into the Ammonoosuc River Valley at Bretton Woods, in the town of Carroll. The trail works its way around to the south of Mt. Deception in the Dartmouth Range, then ascends Cherry Mountain to fine views, and falls into the town of Jefferson. The trail crosses the Jefferson Dome at Cherry Pond and ascends to Jefferson village on Route 2. There it rises into the Pliny Range and runs the high-elevated ridges, over 4,000 feet high at Mt. Waumbek, and crosses into the town of Berlin at Mt. Weeks, and then descends into the town of Lancaster.

On to Kilkenny

The CT soon rises again into the Pilot Range and crosses the summit of Mt. Cabot, again above 4,000 feet, and slips into the wild and beautiful unincorporated township of Kilkenny. From Mt. Cabot the trail rides the north ridge of the Pilot Range to the outstanding summit of The Horn and descends gradually to high mountain ponds to the township of Stark and the Upper Ammonoosuc River valley.

From this point, The Cohos Trail enters the Nash Stream Forest, a recently acquired 39,000-acre parcel of state land filled with a jumble of peaks, valleys, ponds, and cold streams. The trail wanders out of Stark Township near the conspicuous bald twin summits called the Percy Peaks, and enters the town of Stratford. From there, the trail descends to the Nash Stream valley floor, a region that was devastated by a catastrophic flood from a dam breach in 1969. The area is still struggling to reclaim its former grandeur.

In Stratford, the trail reaches the fine summit of Sugarloaf Mt. at 3,701 feet, then moves off to steadily rising and isolated country near 3,610-foot Mt. Muise. The path crosses into the unincorporated township of Odell, then the backcountry of Columbia, and finally rises to the cleared summits of Baldhead South and Dixville Peak at the edge of Dixville township.

In Dixville, the trail tiptoes up to and around the remarkable cliffs of Dixville Notch, and ventures north of the Balsams Grand Resort into chain-pond country, and deep fir and spruce forests. It rises through a mountain notch in southern Stewartstown and levels out at a group of high plateau lakes called the Diamond Ponds.

To Be Continued

From the lakes, the trail exists largely on paper only. It is in the planning stages and will not be completed for several years.

Once built, the northern-most third of the Cohos Trail will likely head in stair-step fashion west northwest around Mudget Mountain, flow north to abandoned hill farms on Ben Young Hill, and enter the region of the headwaters of the Connecticut River at Clarksville and Pittsburg townships.

Once in Pittsburg, the trail will become a tour of big-lake country—the Connecticut Lakes—the largest bodies of water in New Hampshire north of Lake Winnepesaukee. Utilizing woods road, new trail, snowmobile trail, tertiary roads, and state rights of way and the like, the path will wind around Lake Francis, north of First Connecticut Lake, alongside Second Connecticut Lake, Moose Flowage, Third Connecticut Lake, and finally fall into tiny Fourth Connecticut Lake high on the border with Canada and just above the U.S. Customs House. In the future, if plans come to fruition, the trail may continue northeast along the very border between the two countries over Salmon Mountain and Mt. D'Urban toward the boundary marker between New Hampshire, Maine, and Quebec. The Sentiers Frontaliers hiking club of French Quebec wants to cut a link path down to the border from an existing trail not far way.

If the two trails link up, The CohosTrail/Sentiers Frontaliers Trail will become the second major international trail system that we know of in the northeastern United States.

C8C8C8

What And Where Is Coos County?

The Cohos Trail lies entirely in Coos County, New Hampshire, all that is, but the southern-most few hundred feet. Coos County is New Hampshire's northern-most and largest county. It covers an area about the size of Rhode Island, or about three-tenths the size of the Granite State. About as many people live here as live in Rutland, Vermont.

Most visitors to the state either never visit the county or they simply pass through it, as citizens of Quebec often do on their way to Maine's beaches each summer. Those who *do* come to Coos County, come to visit 6,288-foot high Mount Washington, and the Presidential Range, all of which lie in the county's south-eastern corner.

What Do We *Do* Here?

For every 10 people who come to visit the White Mountains, perhaps only one in 10 ever ventures farther north than Route 302 at Bretton Woods or Route 2 at Gorham. There are few tourist attractions in the far north. You have to make your own fun here. The MTV culture doesn't thrive in towns where the only hot spot is the local general store and trees outnumber humans by more than one million to one.

The region has always been remote. After the great Wisconsin glacier retreated 12,000 years ago, this country became a carpet of spruce and fir trees, and a spawning ground for cold, clean rivers that were pristine enough to drink from, rivers we call Connecticut, Ammonoosuc, Magalloway, Androscoggin, Israel, Johns, and Saco. The native Americans who ventured into this area by canoe and dugout boat, stayed only for the summer and fall, settling just long enough to hunt game and harvest berries, wild tubers, and some small riverside plots of maize. In the winter months, even these early peoples left the region for warmer climates closer to the New England coast.

At Beecher Falls, Vermont, just a long jump across the Connecticut River from Stewartstown, New Hampshire, the unofficial low temperature record is 60 below. Balmy 40 below is not unheard of. Zero is an average night temperature from mid-December to mid-February.

Up on the high mountain ridges weather can be frightful, or more accurately—deadly—even in summer. The highest wind gust ever recorded was set in Coos County on Mt. Washington's summit. It was not 150 miles per hour. Not 180. Not even 200. It was 231 miles per hour set during a winter storm in the '30s. In the summer, 100 mile an hour gusts occur often enough to kill.

But enough scare tactics. Coos, spelled "Cohos" by early cartographers and explorers, attracted New England settlers in the late 1700s as lands farther south became harder and harder to purchase as population pressure in the new colonies swelled. Consequently, it's easy to find English town names here, named after Connecticut towns, which were named after the towns of mother England: Stratford, Colebrook, Cambridge, Lancaster, Northumberland, Shelburne.

What's in a Name?

Then there are the towns named after New World and Revolutionary War celebrities: Columbia, Stark, Jefferson. These noble names give way to oddities like Bean's Purchase, Wentworth Location, and Erving's Location, Success, and (Bean again), Bean's Grant. Then these, in turn, give way to place names, and names of distinctive features or human characters, some of fine and some of ill repute (and one I can't repeat here): Hellgate, Devil's Hopyard, Pond of Safety, Dead Diamond, Swift Diamond, and Starr King.

Even some of the mountains in Coos Country come with offhand names, some fascinating, some perplexing: Hedgehog Nubble, Goback, Teapot, Deception, The Bulge, Mitten, Success, Goose Eye, and Rump (whose highest points are actually just over the border in Maine).

But for every tongue-in-cheek name on the Coos County map, there are wonderful tongue twisters, most of which have their origins in Native American languages: Ammonoosuc, Magalloway, Umbagog, Androscoggin, Metalak, Mahoosuc, Waumbek.

Finally, Coos County harbors places that people just couldn't seem to find a proper name for, like Number 3 Mountain, and First, Second, Third, and Fourth Lakes, Unknown Pond, and Lost Nation.

Every four years, Americans of every race and creed find out a little something about this far away place. Every four years there's a race for the nation's highest office and on election eve, the Tillotson family and friends, who make up the entire permanent population of Dixville township—all 20 or so of them—gather together in a European-style hotel in the deep North American woods to vote their preference just as soon as the clock strikes midnight. The national media love this little sidebar and report the first-in-the-nation results faithfully. They always go Republican up there in Dixville. Thank God there are some things you can still count on in this world.

Trees, Only Trees, and More Trees

You can also count on trees in Coos County. And mountains. Lots of them, complete with all their wrinkles: sheer cliffs, waterfalls, boulder gulches, delicious icy streams, bald summit ledges, cold black spruce entanglements, and the smell of balsam fir bows (long since voted into the olfactory hall of fame).

Coos County is square in the middle of two huge overlapping ecosystems—the boreal forest that covers most of the continent north of the Canadian border, and the vast hardwood forests of the eastern United States. Here these two forests mingle as they transform from one system to the other as the traveler moves north.

The county is solidly clothed with trees. About 95 percent of the entire land mass is covered with them. In cold lowland pockets, the primary residents are black spruce, alder, tamarack, and poplar. On the hill and mountain sides, the forest is generally given over to maples, beech, various species of birch and other hardwoods, sometimes mixed well with white pine and hemlock. On the heights, generally above 2,700 feet, the forest gravitates toward the cold hearty upland softwoods, spruce, and fir.

A distinct feature of the plant community in Coos County and only a very few other isolated pockets in the northeast, are the subarctic and true arctic species that grow near or above 4,000 feet where the average annual temperature is very low and competition for growing space and nutrients has been eliminated by the harsh climate.

Some species of plant on the highest zones along The Cohos Trail are not found anywhere else in the east, and their nearest relatives reside as far north as northern Labrador. These plants are so rare that one should use caution when walking at high elevations. Stay on the trail or on rock and avoid any exposed soils or low growing vegetation.

Quiet—Big Quiet

Coos County still harbors the sound of blood in your temples, rushing wind in close-packed red spruce needles, the burbling of countless rivulets of water, and the maniacal laugh of the loon. I've seen snowmobilers turn off their engines on a bald wintry summit and sit and listen to the grand silence. It is the sound of the great continent before the year 1600. The all-silence has been killed off like the eastern mountain lion, and now it reigns in only a tiny fraction of its former range.

The Cohos Trail runs through the very heart of Coos County, right along its central spine. Nowhere on the trail do folks set foot in a town of more than a few hundred people, even though the trail is 160 miles long. Because of this, the trail ought to attract to Coos County the sort of people who will give a damn about just how special a place this great northern forested county really is.

If you know how to get by in remote country when it's too dark to walk outside, and there isn't a McDonald's for 60 miles, then welcome. If you carry your trash out with you and know how to dig a pit toilet, then welcome. If you can eat well without a fire, then welcome. If you can stay dry and warm in a raging sleet storm at 4,000 feet, then welcome. If you don't have the urge to vandalize logging equipment or smash a window of a car at a trailhead, then welcome.

You've come to the right place. Leave your business suit in the dooryard (northern New Hampshire talk for "front yard"), and come along to experience some of the finest wilderness you'll ever want to see!

ෆෆෆ

Weather Extremes of Coos County

The weather in New Hampshire's North Country is notoriously unpredictable, and at times extremely dangerous. It is not unusual for people to die on the high peaks from hypothermia during the summer. Passing showers, high winds, and low summit temperatures are enough to chill hikers so thoroughly that they become disoriented and succumb. Those who venture into the mountains without carrying a full-length head and body plastic poncho, a wool sweater, knit cap, and a windbreaker or parka in a backpack are courting trouble. Take this seriously. Always pack a rain poncho. Always pack a knit cap. Forty percent of all body heat is lost through the head. So put one in the pack. There is an old saying, "If your feet are cold, put on a hat." That is gospel.

More Sage Advice

If you are staying out in the woods overnight, always pack a rain fly with your pup tent. If you like to pack in without a tent and make a lean-to, then make sure you carry a tarp that will cover 100 square feet of space (10' x 10'). Of course, bring a sleeping bag that is rated for the sorts of temperatures you should expect. And if you are going to hike for extended periods on high elevations, bring a parka. Do not go into the backcountry without these essentials.

In the high country, particularly in the far north, in the Presidential Range region and in the Pilot and Pliny Ranges, it can snow on the summits any month of the year. In summer, electrical storms on the heights can be extremely severe. Take shelter under rock overhangs, beside boulders, below treeline—anywhere where you can gain some measure of protection from the elements.

Lightning kills. The chances of being killed or injured on exposed high ground is much greater than on the valley floor. And remember to take off an aluminum frame pack and stow it 200 feet away from you during an intense storm.

Heat kills, too. Always carry plenty of water and take pains to keep well hydrated during strenuous climbing and fast overland travel. In extremely hot weather, hike early in the morning or late in the afternoon. Or at least stay in the cool of the woods. Avoid mid-day heat.

And finally, morning and late night dew can cause a great deal of discomfort if the dew point coincides with chilly night temperatures. A heavy coating of dew can seem like you have been rained on during the night. Remember that poncho? Place it over your sleeping bag if you are sleeping under the stars on a fine cool night. Dew will settle on the poncho and you can shake off the water in the morning.

CRCRCR

The Geology: What You Are Walking On

The rocks beneath a hiker's feet in Coos County are a strange concoction, the result of a colossal collision of continents more than 400 million years ago. About a third of the rock of the county—from the Connecticut River Valley eastward 10 to 20 miles and curving through a narrow 20-mile band of terrain in the vicinity of the Pilot and Pliny mountain ranges—is the remains of what is called the Bronson Hill island archipelago, probably something like the Philippine Islands are today. The Africa tectonic plate rammed this island arc and shoved it westward as that continent drifted and collided with the North American tectonic plate at a time when fish and early amphibians were considered to be the most advanced life forms on earth.

Above the Pilot and Pliny ranges, from Stratford township northward, the rocks and terrain closely resemble the bedrock of northern Vermont and strata further west, all of which is firmly related to the material of the North American plate.

Tectonic Plate? Magma What?

South and east of the Pilot and Pliny ranges, from the city of Berlin down to the very tip of Coos County in Crawford Notch, the rock underlying the bulk of the White Mountains is exotic terrain broken off from the African or European tectonic plate. About 200 million years ago, when the collided continents began to breakup again and the Atlantic Ocean began to form, the massive geological stress accompanying the continental breakup created conditions for mountain building and massive lava outpourings up and down the east coast. The Appalachian Mountain chain, including the White Mountains, was uplifted due to these titanic forces.

Magma intruded great fracture zones in the region, and lava flooded the land, building up a massive highland plateau. Rain, snow, wind, frost, and glacier ice have carved that ancient plateau

37

into the landscape we see today as mountains, hills, valleys, and river courses. So Coos County is an exotic hodgepodge of island debris, home turf, and African leftovers, much of which is covered with magmatic igneous and metamorphic residues, laid down as an afterthought.

The immediate landscape we see today is a direct result of the actions of glacier ice. Not much more than 12,000 years ago, the mile thick Wisconsin Ice Sheet retreated from the region as the climate began to warm up. All over the county and along The Cohos Trail, you can see evidence of the ice, if you know what to look for. Throughout the 160-mile length of The Cohos Trail, trekkers will come across large boulders—called glacial erratics—sitting on the landscape, sometimes hundreds or even thousands of them, large and small, littering the forest. These rocks "dropped out" of the ice sheet as it melted and retreated northward. All over the county there are cliffs, the majority of which face southwest, south, or southeast. These cliffs are often associated with hills and peaks, which have bowling ball-like north sides, ground smooth and round by the massive ice sheet. But as the ice overtopped these heights, the weight and force of the unsupported ice on the southern sides began plucking rocks off south faces, creating cliffs and steep, ledgy southern sides.

Cirques, Drumlins, and Gremlins, too?

In many areas there are mountain bowls or cirques, and U-shaped valleys carved into gentle forms by the ice. There are serpentine mounds called eskers and sand hills (note the sand pits along the way) called drumlins which are the remains of water courses that once flowed beneath the glaciers and then silted up with sand and stone.

There are many bald or "spotty" summits in the county, where soils are absent or so thin that they support little plant life. The glacier ice scoured these summits to bedrock thousands of years ago. These naked heights dry out in the summer and lightning can set fire to the dry brush and new growth trees.

This drought-fire cycle is still at work. The most spectacular example of this is Percy Peaks in the Nash Stream Forest. South Percy is ledgy and spotty with low shrub growth and some trees. But North Percy is a vast expanse of naked granite slabs. The only places where growth can gain a hold are in debris between the slabs. What soil there is can only support blueberry and cinque-foil and a few other hearty, acid-loving plants.

Bogs and fens, some of the lakes in the region, and many of the small round "kettle ponds" in the county have origins in glaciers, too. The ice scooped depressions in the land to create basins for water to fill in. Or huge blocks of ice broke away from the retreating glaciers and remained behind on the landscape. Glacial outwash sediments filled in around the ice blocks and when the ice melted, small ponds formed. Some of these have filled in with vegetation, creating wetlands ideal for wildlife.

CBCBCB

The Economy of Coos County

Coos County's economy is based on forest products and forest recreation. Throughout the length of The Cohos Trail, the trekker will come across logging cuts, young and old, with vegetation growing back at varying heights depending on how recent the harvest has occurred. The forests of Coos County are working forests and have been for 150 years. Fiber from wood chips feeds the region's half dozen paper mills. Whole logs find their way to saw mills and veneer mills.

About 95 percent of the county is clothed in trees. That the county remains entirely wooded is the result of management strategies of large paper companies, and state and federal agencies. In Coos County, large parcel land ownership ensures that the land remains forest, and that many of the lakes and ponds remain development free.

Don't like logging operations? Wait five years and you will have a new forest overtopping your head. The moose and deer will have come in good numbers. How many trees do you see in a Wal-Mart parking lot five years after it was paved?

The timber and paper companies in Coos County have done a good job in keeping the land open for public use as well as keeping it forested.

Today new multiple-use initiatives, and new harvest practices that reduce impact on high elevation terrain, wetlands, and riparian environment, are ensuring the return of certain wildlife and plant species that were extinct in the county as little as a few decades ago.

CECECE

The Spirit of Coos County

Native peoples might revere places such as the mountains and the lakes of Coos County as sacred places, places where the spirit of the ancient rocks, cool air, vast forests, wild animals, and whimsical weather gather to form a whole, noble experience that is a greater entity than the sum of its parts.

The Cohos Trail is a physical pathway, certainly, but it is also a spiritual pathway, a footpath to the human soul.

Don't buy that? Well, who is not moved to the very core sitting alone on a remote mountain summit, lying in the quiet of a dense spruce and fir forest, or languishing beside a roaring mountain cascade.

Like the primordial rhythm of ocean waves on our continent's shores, the vastness and stillness of the North Country seeps, and then pours, into every sense, and moistens and refreshes the arid recesses of our being.

We are, after all, only a very few centuries removed from relying on instincts that all humanity once took for granted for a thousand centuries.

We are hungry to resurrect those instincts, to learn enough about the natural world so that we feel comfortable with ourselves. So we can "go home" to the wild from whence we came and feel at home in the place.

CRCRCR

Wildlife Denizens of the Coos Forests

On The Cohos Trail you will walk and climb through myriad micro-habitats, perhaps the most diverse of any biosystem in northern New England. From arctic tundra to the chilly 120-foot depths of First Connecticut Lake, from black, cold spruce forests in dark bogs, to beautiful wildflower meadows on open mountain slopes, you will drift through a healthy environment that supports a panoply of species.

Since the "cut everything" logging practices of the late 1800s, episodes of devastating forest fires, and two centuries of hardscrabble farming, most of the forest has returned to the hills, valleys and mountains of Coos County. In fact, the county is about 95 percent forested.

The return of the forest has meant that most species that were present in the forest before the arrival of white settlers have returned or at least have partially recovered their original populations. Many mammals, dozens of birds, a handful of hearty reptiles and amphibians, and a good number of native fish, live in the county.

Some very rare animals have been recorded here, including the eastern mountain lion and the bald eagle. Moose have become very common. Black bear are common, as well. Fox, eastern coyote, fisher, beaver, raccoon, porcupine, woodchuck, weasel, mink, skunk, deer, chipmunk, and snowshoe hare abound. Osprey are a frequent sight. Bobcat and otter are less plentiful; lynx are very rare. The wonderful pine marten, a creature that is virtually unknown to most people in the eastern United States, is actually making a comeback here.

Coos County is a bit too far north for oak-loving animals like gray squirrels, but several species of flying squirrel are known in the area, as is the ever-present red squirrel.

Lions, and Bears, And ...

Six snakes and several turtles, including the snapping, painted, and wood turtle, can survive in the region. Numerous toads, salamanders, frogs, peepers, and newts find ways of coping with the long winters. The lakes and streams may possess several species cold and warm water fish, including several species of trout, landlocked salmon, bullhead (horn pout), pickerel, and bass.

The wildlife on The Cohos Trail is its real secret treasure. Here's a limited list of the wild folks you may see on the trail, although we don't list all the 70-odd species of birds, most of the fish, the insects, and all the tiny mammals that are known to inhabit the region. There are persistent reports of eastern mountain lion, but the creatures are thought to be extremely rare and perhaps lone animals that pass through the region infrequently.

- Moose, Whitetail Deer, Black Bear, Pine Marten, Fisher Cat
- Coyote, Tree Frog, Bull Frog, Wood Toad
- Beaver, Muskrat, Raccoon, Porcupine, Otter, Skunk, Weasel
- Snowshoe Hare, Bobcat, Short-eared Bat, Chipmunk
- Bald Eagle, Osprey, Peregrine Falcon, Gray Jay, Loon, Turkey
- Merganzer, Grouse, Blue Heron, White Egret, King Fisher
- Pileated Woodpecker, Wood Duck, Barred Owl, Raven, Snipe

Linda Chestney

An abundance of wildlife inhabits The Cohos Trail region.

- Box Turtle, Painted Turtle, Red-backed Salamander
- Salmon, Horn Pout, Brook Trout, Brown Trout
- Garter Snake, Green Snake, Shrew, Vole, Leech
- Bittern, Star Nosed Mole...
- And of course, that famous and storied menace, the Black Fly

What to Do When You Meet A Moose

The monarch of The Cohos Trail is the moose. You will meet moose on The Cohos Trail if you are on the trail for any real length of time. They are very common, and they like to walk open trails as much as we do. On average, I meet one every day that I walk the trail.

Moose are generally quiet, rather docile animals. In my experience, they will usually stand their ground, perk their big ears forward to listen to you, and keep an eye on you. Sometimes they simply walk away. A female with a calf may stay put and browse or move away quickly. In rare instances, a cow may charge and lash out with her hooves. I have never been charged, but I was almost stepped on while I slept zipped up in my sleeping bag under the stars one night.

Moose can be unpredictable, particularly in mid to late fall—the rutting season. Males move about a great deal during the rut, even late at night. They can become territorial, too, and they will let you know who is boss sometimes by slamming their antlers into brush and small trees. If you encounter a big male in the fall, move quietly and quickly away from it. Several people I know have been in tangles with male moose, and one fellow had his hand crushed when a moose pinned it against a tree.

There are sure signs that a moose is uncomfortable with you. Keep your eyes on the ears. If they lay back, flat for an extended period, the animal is troubled. And if the moose turns its hindquarters to you, that's a defensive measure. Since a moose's hind legs are extremely powerful, it turns its back to you to kick at you. If you were close enough to receive a kick, it could kill you instantly or maim you terribly.

Most of the year, simply stop on the trail, and slowly backup a bit if you think you are too close. If there is a clump of trees about, you might work your way to them and put the trees between you and the moose. Avert your eyes. Do not stare into the eyes of the animal. Exhibit browsing behavior—look like you are nibbling the foliage. This is behavior that moose view as normal and passive. And finally, make a broad detour around the creature and continue on your way.

Over the years I have learned how to stay in close proximity with the great animals without provoking them, but to be truthful, I am never really sure what they will do. If they keep their ears forward and continue to sniff the air in your direction, they are curious and are trying to find out what you are. Since they do not see particularly well, they may take steps toward you to try to get a look at you if they aren't receiving enough information through their other senses.

When they do come forward, I always take a step in the opposite direction, trying to keep a reasonable distance. This seems to be reassuring to moose—and I emphasize "seems." Moving slowly and in plain sight is always the best strategy. And finally, if you are camping alone or with one or two other people, stay out of flat open areas where there are signs that moose bed down at night. Look for large flattened spots in the grasses and weeds. Look for small dugout depressions in the ground, called moose wallows. And look for obvious moose trails. They are very good at making highways in the woods that they travel on regularly. Stay away from these areas.

You do not want to be in the position I was in one late September night, when I bedded down in grasses at the edge of a large meadow, but not far enough away from a moose trail. A big bull came to investigate in the middle of a very dark night and came within feet of stepping on me. The encounter lasted perhaps three minutes at most. I must say, being confined in a sleeping bag under the stars with a 1,400-pound bull moose within spitting distance is a heart-stopping experience—very non-virtual, mind you. I never want to be in such tight quarters again, and neither do you. I'm just plain lucky I did not get stepped on.

But I do love my typical encounters with moose. I very much look forward to meeting them. On the Cohos Trail, if you know what to do, you will likely have an experience of a lifetime when you and a moose have a chance encounter.

What to Do if You Meet A Bear

Black bears in northern New Hampshire are fairly common and very shy creatures. In Coos County there is no record of anyone ever being hurt by a black bear. In virtually every case, black bear will leave the area you are walking in. Your chances of actually seeing a bear are rather remote. In 20 years of bush-whacking by myself in Coos County, I have never encountered a bear in its normal habitat. I have only seen them through my truck windshield as they cross roads.

If, on the very, very rare chance that you are charged by a bear, such as a female with cubs, the bear will run at you in a bluff attempt to scare you away. The scare tactic works, of course. The bear avoids a real confrontation, and you do, too. And do the other sensible thing. Store your food in a duffel bag suspended from a narrow tree branch out of easy reach of the black bear (they can climb trees). And don't leave any food or food drip-pings or residue at all for them to find.

Most bears in Coos County are not acclimated to humans. They do not associate humans with food. That's the way it should be. Once a bear learns that humans are an easy source to gain access to food, a bear can become a nuisance, and worse, danger-ous.

But please, black bears are not grizzly bears. They are much, much smaller than their brown cousins, and have considerably different temperaments. Do not panic if you see one. Consider yourself very lucky and even honored.

What To Do If You Meet Homo Sapiens

I like to think that people in the woods are at far greater risk from other people than they are from any of the wildlife. On the Cohos Trail, you will see other people infrequently, particularly in the regions north of the Presidential Range. In some of the more remote areas, you are unlikely to see people at all for many, many miles.

But humans can be more unpredictable than moose. Let me give you a sobering example. Many years ago I parked an old VW bus beside a Buick Riviera at a lonely trailhead to Mt. Moosilauke on the southern edge of the White Mountain Na-tional Forest. I slept overnight near the summit of the fine peak, spent the morning above 4,000 feet, and came down to drive home by 1 p.m. that day.

When I reached the trailhead, the Buick had been savaged. Two windows were completely smashed, and of course, the big, new radio/tape player or something or other had been ripped from the dash.

What do I do? I leave my truck unlocked and don't have a fancy tape system to pluck. I leave nothing in the cab except some litter, so my truck looks like I'm a slob, not a well-heeled suburbanite.

ﬄﬄﬄ

Woods Ethics

A century ago, North Country people who went into remote lands carried with them an unwritten code of woods ethics that one wouldn't think of violating. The idea was if you went into the woods, you left it just as it was before you went in. If you used remote property, such as a well-stocked cabin, a boat, a pile of split, dry wood, you left the property just as you found it and you replaced the wood you burned, or the flour you used to make your dinner biscuit.

If you use a camp or other resource on a trail, leave it in better condition than when you found it. If a facility or sign or bridge is damaged, report it so someone can fix it. If someone has left trash behind, carry it out.

Everyone should learn these unwritten rules. Everyone should give a damn. Local people live this way. Learn to respect this wonderful, timeless tenet.

Carry In, Carry Out

Leave nothing behind in the woods that is not readily biodegradable.

Carry out all trash and even pick up trash if you find it in the woods. Carry a plastic trash bag with you at all times so that it can be handy for depositing trash to be carried out.

Respect Private Property

The Cohos Trail exists because private landowners and state and federal officials have permitted you to move through their lands and public lands. If you despoil the property, you threaten the very existence of this long, beautiful trail.

Therefore, we ask that you be an exemplary citizen on these lands, and that you report any and all abhorrent behavior to local, state, and federal authorities.

And go a step further. If you see someone creating a problem do not reprimand him or her. Instead, take it upon yourself to educate them as to why they must refrain from the activity they are engaged in. Make the troublemaker a friend of the CT, not an enemy.

Stay on the Trail

The Cohos Trail crosses some fragile ecosystems, particularly high-elevation environments, and in and around bogs and other wetlands. Stay on the trail in these areas to minimize damage to local flora and fragile soil. On bald summits and ledges, please pick your way along on rocks to avoid the rare arctic and subarctic plants that often grow in these areas where little else can.

Trail Signage and Blazes

The Cohos Wilderness Trail is a reasonably well-marked trail. There should be little trouble following the right of way.

But unlike most trails that are blazed (painted patches on trees and rocks) with one color of paint, the CT is a 160-mile right-of-way that uses a number of existing trails that are signed and blazed with various paint colors.

About 95 percent of Cohos county is solidly clothed with trees.

Where the CT is the only existing right-of-way, it is marked with yellow paint. North of the White Mountain National Forest lands, *any* yellow blaze is a CT blaze. Where the CT is a part of White Mountain National Forest trails, it uses the existing marks, often yellow, white, or even robin-egg-blue paint blazes. The Kilkenny Ridge Trail, and Starr King Trail are blazed in light yellow paint, not much different than that of the CT. The Davis Path blazes are light blue.

The state of New Hampshire maintains boundary lines in a straightforward blue color—often in large patches and in association with ax blazes. Timber companies may use orange, red, or other colors.

International Paper Company blazes are orange, and you will see them often between Kelsey Notch and Mt. Muise.

Blazes may be painted on trees, posts, rocks on the ground, bedrock slabs, or on stacks of rocks called cairns.

At each important junction (where confusion my arise) outside of the White Mountain National Forest, you will find a little CT sign, which is a small, dark brown wood plaque with machine-routed letters painted in yellow. These signs are a slightly elongated square that sport two cutout peaks on top. They are a very simple, rustic representation of the outline of the Percy Peaks. They are inconspicuous except for the bright yellow CT letters.

One of the hallmarks of the CT is its lack of signage. The Cohos Trail Association decided that the trail should be a rather basic, no-nonsense wilderness hike, and that trailblazers would not "paint the woods" every few feet and put up signs everywhere about everything. So signage and blazing is sparse, but adequate.

Most of the time, single blazes are spaced 300 to 500 feet apart. And signs may be a mile or even several miles apart, except near junctions.

The CT uses one other time-honored form of trail marking—the rock cairn. In a dozen places along the trail where its more feasible to have a ground marker than a sign in a tree or on a post, the CT employs small stacks of stones placed atop one another. These are usually marked with yellow paint.

CBCBCB

Other Recreational Uses

This guide has been written primarily for the hiker or snowshoer. But there are sections of The Cohos Trail which are well suited to other uses, and there are some right of ways which are already used for other purposes.

Trail Bikes and Road Bikes

Trail bikes, under human foot power, are ideally suited for the numerous Nash Stream Forest roads, including Nash Stream Main Road, Westside Road, Trio Ponds Road, Picnic Loop, and Jimmy Cole Road. Between Bretton Woods and Jefferson, on the east side of Cherry Mountain, runs the Old Cherry Mt. Road, a long dirt service road that is a delight for pedalers, particularly the bog under beautiful Mt. Deception.

The Balsams Grand Resort Hotel in dramatic Dixville Notch maintains extensive biking trails and rents excellent equipment. Champion International Corp. has designated nearly 75 miles of woods road as compatible with trail bikes, including the fascinating East Inlet Road which runs from Second Connecticut Lake for 15 miles into the very northeastern-most corner of the state. You can't get farther away than up near Boundary Pond and Mt. D'Urban hard by the Quebec line.

To obtain the Ross Hunter Map of the Connecticut Lakes Region's recreational trails, contact the M/S Printing Company at Colebrook, New Hampshire.

Trekkers on road bikes can shadow The Cohos Trail in the valleys on the few long and isolated highways and secondary roads of Coos County. Both Route 110 and Route 26 feature splendid scenery and few cars. And Route 3 from First Connecticut Lake to the border is a must, particularly in the early morning and at dusk when moose always frequent the roadsides.

Nicolin Fields Publishing, Inc., which published this book, prints several fine trail biking titles featuring rides in Nash Stream Forest and other regions of Coos County.

Cross Country Skiing

Cross Country skiers who don't mind following skimobile track can move over dozens of miles of country along the CT. The Balsams Grand Resort maintains dozens of miles of well-groomed trail in the Dixville Notch region between Mud Pond and Dixville Peak. Their system is among the most challenging, most diverse, and most beautiful in the entire East. And the Bretton Woods Corp. maintains a mountain full of cross-country trails too, in the valley beneath Mt. Washington, Mt. Eisenhower, and Mt. Deception.

A word of caution. For years there has been a little friction between snowmobilers and cross-country skiers. In many back country areas, skimobilers have built and maintained—with their own hands and dollars—extensive trail systems. Cross-country skiers should be mindful of this. I'm a cross-country skier exclusively, but I never fail to raise a friendly wave to skimobilers running on trails *they* built, that *I* use.

Contact the Balsams at Dixville Notch for their beautifully detailed cross-country map of their system. Or contact the Bretton Woods Company in Bretton Woods for a copy of their trail system.

Rock Climbing

There are several rock faces on the CT suitable for rock or ice climbing. They include Giant Stairs, the small ledges in Devil's Hopyard, Rogers Ledge, and Devil's Slide in Stark village not too far off the trail. Some of the friable cliffs in Dixville Notch have attracted a few climbers, and the vertical east side of Mt. Magalloway is a natural, but it's so remote that it is rarely climbed.

Mineral Collecting

Rock hounds, those folks who scour rock formations for common or rare gemstones, crystals, and minerals, may find a great deal of new land to prospect opened up by the CT. Coos County's neighbor to the east is Oxford County, Maine, long famous among eastern rock hounds for its deposits of semiprecious gemstones, particularly tourmaline.

Rock hounding is permitted on state lands provided the only tools used are small non-powered hand tools. On North Percy there is ample evidence that the gem hunters have been at work with rock chisel and hammer.

Wildlife Viewing

The Cohos Trail offers trekkers a good chance to see all sorts of wildlife in its natural habitat. The largest mammal in North America, the moose, is common and often seen along the trail right of way and along roads that have been salted over the winter. Moose crave the sodium in the salt.

Biggest isn't always best. There are over 60 species of birds, including the rare peregrine falcon, osprey, and bald eagle that live along the route, as well as more than 20 mammals, a few reptiles, and amphibians. So bring binoculars. And learn to sit quietly for extended periods of time. You will be rewarded.

The state recently built a wildlife interpretive walk just east of Dixville Notch Wayside. It's an interesting stop for families and for those unfamiliar with the fauna of the north.

Snowmobiling

Some stretches of The Cohos Trail—particularly along Nash Stream Main Road, Sugarloaf Arm, Kelsey Notch, Dixville Peak, and trails north of the Balsams to Murphy Dam—are existing and often well-maintained skimobile trails. Some routes in Pittsburg's far north are snowmobile trails also. Parts of CT ride over the Number 5 snowmobile corridor, the longest, continuous snowmobile trail in New Hampshire.

Numerous North Country clubs publish maps of the trails they have built and take care of. Many can be obtained from the New Hampshire Snowmobile Association with offices at Concord, New Hampshire, and from local general stores in the North Country. (The Diamond Peaks General Store on Rte. 26 just west of Dixville Notch has more good maps than the armed forces.)

Snowshoeing

The entire Cohos Trail is suitable for snowshoeing, with the exception of very steep areas and some of the more remote sections that would be tough to get in and out of during the short daylight hours of winter.

I snowshoe portions of the trail often, because it is usually unearthly quiet and peaceful and it's easy to see by their tracks what the animals of the forest have been doing. I also enjoy getting a good workout in bracing, icy cold temperatures.

Over the last decade, snowshoe technology has improved considerably on the old way of getting around in the woods. Some models can grip ice; some are suitable for running. Trying doing that for any length of time with the early gut baskets!

Winter Camping

In winter, the rules change. Fire is not a threat to the forests in winter, so winter camping is not so much of a taboo. Few people ever camp out in the forests of Coos County anyway. Most folks who do, do so high on the slopes of the Presidential Range.

But winter camping has its rewards far from the Whites. Lesser summits have dropped their leaves and views lost in summer return in winter. Summits in light or moderate snowfalls are enchanting. And there is no word in the English language for the sight of the night sky on a cold Coos winter evening.

If you venture out on The Cohos Trail for extended periods during the winter months, you have to be prepared for arctic-like conditions.

Temperatures can drop to minus 40 degrees on those nights when a monstrous Canadian high pressure system descends. The wind ceases altogether, and the mercury in the thermometer on the porch drops like an elevator with a broken cable in a New York skyscraper.

Besides the great layers of clothing and Everest sleeping bag, you must carry a compass in the event you find yourself in a heavy snowfall, or worse, a blizzard. If you lose the trail, a compass will at least allow you to choose a course and stick to it instead of wandering in whiteout conditions in a forest that now looks like its populated with anorexic ghosts.

Bushwhacking

The time-honored art of bushwhacking is taking a back seat to the GPS (Global Positioning System, a sophisticated, high tech "compass" guiding system) craze these days. With a day's wages you, too, can link up to your nearest neighborhood satellite and find out exactly where you are. In Coos County, leave the GPS gee-whiz stuff home. Okay?

All you need is a good compass and a topo map and you can have fun all day rooting around in the wilds, using the CT as a launching pad to explore the unknown places. Then you should be able to find your way back to the trail without incident.

Or use the oldest method of all—counting. Count how many ridges you go over and streams you cross. Every few minutes stop, turn around and look at the landmarks behind you, and memorize what you see. Then when you want to go back the way you came in, you'll recognize the place and you'll be able to count off the streams and ridges you've crossed.

Swimming and Diving

There is every opportunity to take a plunge along the CT, be it in clear streams, cold lakes, warm ponds, beneath a waterfall, or in the backwaters with the big leeches of Coos County. And there are challenging places to scuba dive, as well, particularly in the Connecticut Lakes Region. Lake Francis harbors the remains of a drowned town.

Canoeing, Kayaking, and Tubing

The lakes and ponds of Coos County are ideal for canoeing. Many possess unseen backwater inlets that are wildlife havens. And because you can drift up to these quiet spots without making a sound, you are often rewarded with glimpses of creatures you cannot see any other way. Canoers can work the Ammonoosuc in places, the Israel River, the Upper Ammonoosuc, and lots of the Connecticut River and Androscoggin. Kayakers like the flatwater too, but it's the fast water that is dear to their hearts. The famous Androscoggin River is some miles to the east of The Cohos Trail. It is a magnet for kayakers.

Along the CT, expert kayakers can attempt portions of Nash Stream in high water, or Clear Stream on the east side of Dixville Notch or the Mohawk River on the west side of the notch. Portions of the Upper Ammonoosuc and Ammonoosuc Rivers have fast water, too. Tubing is for everyone and there are a few hot spots. People often tube the Upper Ammonoosuc River when it's running swiftly after good rains from Bell Hill Bridge through Stark village. Gentle rapids above the beautiful Stark covered bridge make the trip a memorable one. Nash Stream sometimes hosts a tuber or two, but the best place for running is just south of the Nash Stream Forest boundary to its junction with the Upper Ammonoosuc. Above this area the stream is too dangerous in high water, particularly in the area of the Westside Road Bridge.

All-Terrain Vehicles

ATVs are not suited to running on The Cohos Trail or any other natural trail system, in my mind. Unlike snowmobiles, ATVs impact the environment severely and devastate footways and habitat. Snowmobilers build and expertly maintain extensive trail systems that many recreators use. ATVs quickly degrade those systems. In my experience, the riders of ATVs generally do not organize to maintain trails, probably because the task of keeping long stretches of ATV trails in good condition is impossible. Therefore it is not possible to condone their use on The Cohos Trail system.

There are exceptions, however. ATVs do allow disabled people to enjoy backcountry environs. That's a good thing. And sensible ATV riders, who confine their sport to built-up gravel ways that can support the machines without degrading the soils, have a place in the north.

ଔଔଔ

PART I

The Montalban Whites

When Not To Dedicate A Mountain

Stories from the Back Woods

My first real assignment as a newspaper writer: cover Julie Nixon Eisenhower as she, like magic, turns Mt. Pleasant in the Presidential Range, into Mt. Eisenhower.

I was on a school bus with 20 other reporters, most of them from big dailies. I was a rookie on the smallest paper ever incorporated to print newsprint. We were being shuffled from the Mt. Washington Hotel to the site of the dedication. And it was pouring rain. The wipers on the bus were on full force. The driver had a difficult time seeing. Worse, winds were gusting to 35 miles per hour outside. The temperature was in the mid-40s.

On a small bluff alongside Route 302 just east of Bretton Woods, the state had built a tiny memorial to the late president. We had to walk 200 feet uphill to a spot where a tent had been erected and a canvas thrown over something sizable at one end of the tent. There were dozens of chairs under the roof fabric, but the reporters were not permitted to sit in any of them. They were reserved for guests and for the Secret Service.

When it Rains...

It was 2 p.m., but it was dark as dusk and monochrome with sheet rain. Northern New Hampshire's mountains are famous for such days of misery. When they last for four or five days, domestic violence rates surge, whiskey purchases at the State liquor stores increase three fold, and people make up their minds once and for all to move away. In the gloom, Julie Nixon Eisenhower arrived under a fleet of umbrellas. The tent filled to capacity, and the reporters were edged out to the very perimeter of the tent. I was behind the last row of seats where a tent pole

58

didn't quite have enough muscle to keep the river of water above from depressing the tent fabric and delivering a frigid shower down my back in periodic pulses of, oh say, once a minute.

Things were happening quickly. Flash bulbs were popping. Someone up front had a walkie-talkie and was yelling into it. Seems there was a climber on top of Mt. Pleasant armed with a hand radio too, and a metal plaque inscribed with the words "Mt. Eisenhower." This hiker—lost to us in a full blown hurricane well above timberline on the 4,761 foot summit—was right on cue. Amazing.

In a minute, he was going to change Mt. Pleasant into something greater. When the tipsy party who first named the peaks ran out of presidents to honor, they pointed to the big bald dome on the Southern Presidential Range, and because they were feeling rather pleasant from imbibing a pint of Oh Be Joyful, named the peak for their physical state at the time. Now the peak was going to be named for the very American who saved the world for democracy.

All for the Sake of History?

Splash. More water down my back. My underwear was soaked. My pants drenched. Julie said something. Someone said something else, and the big canvas tarp over the obelisk was whisked away—and there, in the half light—was a big granite rock with a bronze plaque bolted to it. More flash pops. At the same moment, the hiker in the hurricane on the summit bolted his plaque to a rock cairn and, presto... Mt. Eisenhower.

Then everyone was gone. In an instant. The storm had not abated, and the little party on the knoll was chilled to the bone. Me? I was suffering hypothermia and swearing that I would never vote Republican as long as I lived.

The next day, the morning dawned crystalline. Newly minted Mt. Eisenhower stood out in the morning sun in all its newfound glory. Julie, back in Washington, didn't see it. I was in bed with a cold. I didn't see it either. I never went back anyway, to the little knoll with the bronze plaque on the granite rock. I pass by it quite a bit, but I never stop.

Damned if I ever will.

CRCRCR

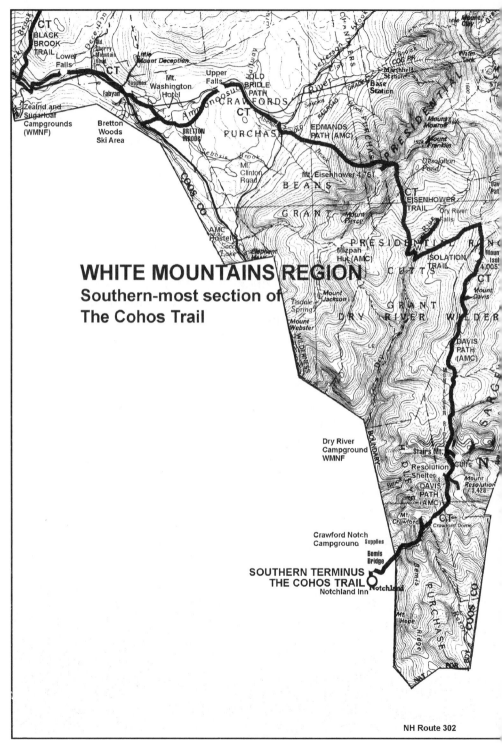

WHITE MOUNTAINS REGION
Southern-most section of
The Cohos Trail

NH Route 302

SOUTHERN TERMINUS OF THE COHOS TRAIL

First Leg:
The Montalban Whites

Where To? What Next?

This section of the guidebook begins the step-by-step or play-by-play account of the actual system of existing and abandoned foot trails, skidder tracks, gated wagon ruts, traveled routes, old cinder rail beds, and moose "highways" that comprise The Cohos Trail (CT). This guide section begins at the Southern Terminus, at the Davis Path trailhead in Hart's Location, New Hampshire, and works its way northward approximately 160 trail miles.

To begin the arduous journey over the central elevated spine of Coos County, New Hampshire, you must find your way to Notchland over five miles south of Crawford Notch State Park on Route 302. From the south, from Conway and North Conway, travel northbound on Route 302, through Bartlett village and beyond Attitash/Bear Peak ski areas, around the great sweeping dogleg in the Saco River and north until you see the Notchland Inn on the left (west) side of the road. The Davis Path trailhead is exactly opposite the Inn.

From the north, travel 302 southbound from Twin Mountain, along the Ammonoosuc River. Pass Bretton Woods ski area and the Mt. Washington Hotel. Eventually swing into the great chasm that is Crawford Notch. Travel 5.5 miles beyond the Crawford Notch State Park visitor's center. Pass Dry River Campground and Crawford Notch General Store and Campground on the left, then look for the Notchland Inn on the right a mile south. Directly across the highway from the Notchland is the Davis Path trailhead.

Pull into the large parking area and park. Walk north through the lot to a tire track alongside Route 302 to the Bemis Bridge. This is the starting point of The Cohos Trail.

The Davis Path

The Cohos Trail uses existing White Mountain National Forest trails for the first third of its journey north. The first trail you encounter and stay on for many hours is the Davis Path, built by Nathaniel P.T. Davis beginning in 1844 as the third and by far the longest bridle path to the summit of Mt. Washington. The trail uses the lengthy Montalban Ridge, a high elevation shoulder of Mt. Washington, which carries such peaks as Mt. Resolution, Stairs Mt., Mt. Davis, and 4,005-foot Mt. Isolation, and a westerly spur—Bemis Ridge—which supports the fine little bald summit of Mt. Crawford and several lesser peaks.

That this bridle path was built at all and remained open for a dozen years is testimony to the doggedness of Mr. Davis. Mt. Resolution is named for his tenacity in the face of what seems to us as daunting and futile a task as any one man could undertake. Without Davis' attention, the path fell into disuse, but in 1910 it was reopened by the Appalachian Mountain Club and has remained open and well maintained under the AMC's guidance.

Bemis Bridge

The Cohos Trail (CT) begins with a step onto a bit of human ingenuity and engineering—the Bemis Bridge. This is a long, narrow span over the Saco River. It is an honest-to-goodness homespun suspension bridge with a treadway wide enough to accommodate one person at a time.

Two steel post towers rise on each bank of the Saco, and two spun steel cables stretch out and hold up each side of the planks that create the walkway. The cables are attached to cross beams beneath the planking by stout steel rods.

The whole structure has a pleasing human scale to it and is a joy to stand on. In the middle of the bridge, there is a fine view up the gravelly Saco to the Frankenstein Cliffs. The span is a private structure, so leave a small donation in the little wooden barrel nailed to the highway-side of the span.

The Bemis Bridge marks the southern terminus of The Cohos Trail. If you've been hiking south from far up-country, this is the end of the journey.

To Mount Crawford (3,129 Feet)

Cross the Bemis Bridge and enter a field on private land near a camp. Turn left and enter the woods, crossing a stream and a dry bed a couple of times before the trail reaches the boundary of the White Mountain National Forest. Here the trail begins to climb in earnest. As the path moves eastward it soon passes out of Carroll County, New Hampshire and into the political entity that is vast Coos County. The trail remains in Coos County the entire way north.

Where the trail crosses into Coos County, it links with the actual old bridle path that Nathaniel Davis built. The path rides on some of the original fill and stone that Davis brought in. The trail follows this once well-built way, swinging back and forth as it encounters steeper and steeper terrain. This uphill two-mile push jogs along the spur Bemis ridgeline that links with the massive Montalban Ridge. As the two-mile mark approaches, a series of bare ledges appears and views open to the southwest to the Nancy Ponds territory, Mt. Carrigan and Tripyramid. It's a just reward after the long uphill grind.

Giant stairs just off the Davis Path.

Immediately the hiking becomes easier as you can now ridge run for many miles. Work northward and shortly intersect with a spur trail that isn't readily apparent on the left at the base of a pitched ledge. There is a small wooden sign in the trees, but from below you can miss the sign. Keep left, however, and continue to climb uphill three-tenths of a mile to the remarkable summit of little Mt. Crawford, standing a modest 3,129 feet tall.

The petite peak's heights are a series of crags and ledges with no obstacles blocking the view. A grand panorama opens up in every direction. Mt. Crawford is famous for its perch above the maw of Crawford Notch. The real dimensions of the glacier-gouged valley and the sheerness of its cliffs are in plain sight. The view into the depths to the north is breathtaking.

Mt. Crawford is a preview to many of the unknown and little-climbed peaks of Coos County. So many summits far removed from the Presidential Range reveal whole new vistas and whole new worlds for hikers. So early on Mt. Crawford does us all a favor on the long march toward Canada. It gives us a solid and dramatic idea of what's to come far away to the north.

On the summit of Mt. Crawford, you can trace the serpentine Montalban Ridge, as it rises and sweeps away toward the 6,000 foot "lawns" below Mt. Washington's summit cone. In the foreground is bowler-shaped Mt. Resolution, with its slide-pocked flanks. Just to the left is Stairs Mountain with its bizarre geology. Beyond Stairs, the ridge undulates up and down until it spikes twice out of sight, first at Mt. Davis and then again at the first 4,000-footer on the CT, Mt. Isolation. Beyond, and filling the northern horizon, are the lofty uplands of the northern Presidential Range.

Crawford Dome

From Mt. Crawford, descend the way you came on the main trail and watch for the sign and trail on the left 1,500 feet below the heights. Turn left (north) and meander down through a softwood-lined col and then rebound up and over the broad rounded ledges of a feature called Crawford Dome.

Soil doesn't stick to Crawford Dome. Its surface is a series of baldpates of sizable dimension pocked with an odd assortment of glacial erratic stones and boulders, all of which look lonesome and out of place.

Glance back over your shoulder here for a look at the little pyramidal peak you just descended from. Under the west side (right) of the summit of Mt. Crawford you can make out the little peak's resident gargoyle—a slab of rock that looks like the head of a monitor lizard or even better, a meat-eating dinosaur.

Mt. Resolution (3,428 Feet)

Walk another mile of rather level ridge in and out of scrub and move around the northwestern flank of Mt. Resolution, named for Davis' resolute determination to complete the bridle path to Mt. Washington. Soon the Parker Trail exists right (east) uphill off the Davis Path, on its way to Mt. Langdon and the village of Bartlett. A spur trail exists left at the same spot and falls 300 feet to Resolution shelter, a lean-to structure that will be removed entirely by the USFS when it ages sufficiently to need major repairs. Not far behind the shelter there is reliable water except in the driest of seasons. It's the last reliable water on the Montalban Ridge, so take advantage of it now.

To obtain a viewpoint from Mt. Resolution, walk about half a mile up the Parker Trail ascending moderately all the way. The footway passes close to the summit of Resolution where the trail leads to expansive open ledges that afford fine sweeping vistas over the mountain's raw slabs and talus deposits.

Then return to the Davis Path, turn right (north) and approach one of the more curious summits in all the White Mountains: Stairs Mountain.

Stairs Mountain (3,460 Feet)

Stairs Mountain is a ridge-like formation rising up out of the Montalban uplands. This ridge ends very abruptly at a series of double cliffs one above the other, well named as Giant Stairs. The Giant Stairs are visible from many points in the Whites. Viewed from Mt. Crawford, the Giant Stairs is such an outlandish bit of real estate that there is a small, but happy, band of Giant Stairs loyalists out there who rank it among their favorite spots in the Whites.

Between Mt. Resolution and Stairs Mt., the Davis Path is a beautiful wooded, high ridge walk that is never strenuous. It passes several small rivulets where good water can be obtained most of the time. The Davis Path eventually dips into a shady col, where the Stairs Col Trail breaks away right (east) for Rocky Branch stream. The main trail splits off and begins climbing immediately northwest, slabbing steep terrain under the long ridge of Stairs Mt. After climbing steeply with a few hand and foot scrambles, the trail swings eastward, rises in a series of switchbacks, and approaches the summit ridge. Just before the height of land, a short spur runs out to the Down-Look. All you have to do is glimpse past your feet on the very edge of a near sheer cliff to understand the source of this place name.

It's a short jaunt to a junction. The Davis Path reaches the height of land and drifts left, while the spur trail to Giant Stairs cuts right. Run on level ground through softwoods for 1,000 feet to the great ledges and sheer drops on upper Giant Stairs. There is little room to play about on the narrow ledges of rock, but there are stunning views over about 240 degrees.

The great cliff faces southward and picks up direct sunlight all day. The rock faces warm up by mid-afternoon and the ledges can be pleasantly warm even on cool days. It's a delight to lay back and relax, so much so that I have fallen asleep right on the cliff edge.

Mt. Davis (3,840 Feet)

Leave Stairs Mt. behind and move north again down the long northbound ridge of the mountain. Pass the junction you reached earlier on the left now and move away north on gently descending trail.

As you leave Stairs Mt., you'll notice that the path narrows a bit as fewer and fewer people come this way. The way also exhibits more debris and less erosion control as it gets progressively more remote. The way to Mt. Davis runs on a gently undulating ridge line, lined with spruce, birch, and sprinkled with a few pockets of shrub that can stand acid soil and wet feet. Bottom out in a col and begin a ridge-running dance on ever higher ground for what seems like several miles as the footway ascends the western side of Mt. Davis' southern ridge. Every few thousand feet, the trail passes a small brook or spring (unreliable water) but even these rivulets die away as the trail increases in altitude.

With Mt. Davis at hand, look for a spur trail to the right (east) for a short run to the summit. On the spotty ledges on the heights, most of the realm of the Montalban Range becomes visible. The massive shoulders of the ridge, with the frequent summits popping up like armor plates, run away south from where you have just come. In the opposite direction the lone sentinel that is Mt. Isolation, stands guard, set apart from the southern Presidentials by the Dry River gulf. Mt. Davis boasts one of the very finest views in all the mountains, but its northern neighbor does it one better.

Mt. Isolation (4,005 Feet)

From whichever direction you approach Mt. Isolation, you have come a long, long way to get to the much loved but infrequently climbed peak. Since it is so removed from the mainstream, the aptly named summit sees less traffic than all the other major summits in Mt. Washington's circle of lofty friends. If it were not on the list of 4,000-footers, it would probably see precious few visitors at all.

Leave Mt. Davis and return to the Davis Path. Turn right (north) and descend quickly to a col between Davis and Isolation. Rebound out of the col and regain 400 feet of vertical elevation. The trail threads just below the summit and continues north. Watch carefully for the side to the left. Chase up it and break out onto the clear summit slabs.

Most well-heeled trekkers in the Whites list Isolation as one of the best of all summits. Spin around, there are views at every turn. Most all the major mountain ranges in the region are revealed, with wave after wave of blue ridges washing away to the horizon as far away as the lakes region: the Franconias, the Twin-Bonds complex, Sandwich Range, Carter-Moriah, The Presidentials, Speckled-Caribou, and more. Stirring!

Better yet, there are rarely people here. The summit is usually wind-whistle quiet, giving the trekker a full sense of the lonesome spirit of the place. There is no steady stream of trampers as on the southern Presidentials, yet the Crawford Path with its heavy pedestrian load is only a tall ridgetop away.

Isolation stands high over the Dry River ravine, a deep V-shaped gash in the southwest flank of Presidentials. The great gully effectively cuts off Isolation from Mt. Eisenhower, where you are headed, making it necessary to make a great Z-shaped detour in the northerly flow of the CT.

Dry River

Push off north from Isolation and descend to the ridgeline. The trail continues to rise in elevation along the ridge and in half a mile passes the old site of the Isolation Shelter, long since torn down, and a junction with the Isolation Trail coming up from Rocky Branch from the east (right). If you are running low on water, you may descend the Isolation Trail to the right a considerable distance to find water most of the year.

The Davis Path and the Isolation Trail run together for less than half a mile, then the Isolation trail cuts obliquely left (southwest) while the Davis Path continues for higher ground. The Cohos Trail runs on the back of this western jog down the Isolation Trail footway making for Dry River.

For a short stretch the Isolation Trail runs level on the Montalban Ridge, but soon pitches off the uplands and descends rapidly at a modestly steep grade southwest into the ravine carved by the Dry River. The sound of fast moving water fills the woods, and finally the trail converges with the Dry River Trail, an old slide-eroded logging road here, northeast bound for Lake of the Clouds. Turn abruptly right on the Dry River Trail and follow the waters on the high eastern bank to a clearing that affords a fine view of the rugged river valley. A short while later the Eisenhower Trail breaks off left (north) steeply downhill and fords the river, the first reliable and fast moving water on the CT for at least 10 miles. To reach Mt. Eisenhower, drop down to the river, but wait, less than half a mile away up Dry River is the highest elevation waterfall in the White Mountains, complete with its topside kettle pothole.

Dry River Falls

Leave Mt. Eisenhower to its own devices for now. Climb past the Mt. Eisenhower Trail junction following the Dry River Trail uphill. After 1,000 feet, watch for a spur path to the left downhill. This little footway brings you to a bucolic pool at the base of a modest falls that can be a fat spraying torrent in high water. From the pool you can scramble up the rocks to the top of the falls and plunk yourself into a little kettle hole (if you can stand the perpetually chilly water), chiseled out by stones swirling round and round in a natural depression.

If you are in dire need of shelter in this region, you may continue northeastward on the Dry River Trail to Dry River shelter, nearly a mile uphill from the falls. Otherwise, descend to the junction with the Mt. Eisenhower Trail.

Mt. Eisenhower Trail

At the junction with the Mt. Eisenhower Trail drop down (right if coming downhill, left if coming uphill), and descend steeply on an old right of way, keeping to the most well-worn track amidst some spur offshoots. The path reaches Dry River and crosses at a rocky ford.

Dry River belies its name. It is a quick and turbulent little river and can be impossible to get across in late spring and during sudden mountain storms. Don't underestimate the force of the water here if there has been wet weather. This can be one of the most dangerous spots on the entire CT.

Scramble up the northwest bank and pace downstream well above the bank until it meets a steep, old logging track and turns sharply right and northward uphill quickly away from Dry River. Near the height of the sharp grade, the Dry River Cutoff spins away to the left (south) making for the AMC's big Mizpah Springs Hut several miles away.

Bear straight uphill and the grade slackens, then mount a south ridge between Mt. Eisenhower and Mt. Franklin. The trail rises moderately along this geography near the ridgeline, dodging out of the increasing boreal forest to small bare ledges and blowdowns to offer an occasional view.

Soon the crest of the ridge that carries the southern Presidentials looms. The trail pitches steeply uphill in sweet spruce and fir (their rich fragrance given up by the heat of the sun on the warm south-facing slope). The grade quiets down, patches of ledge appear and the low, cold forest gives way to wind-sheered scrub marking the advent of timberline.

The trail levels out above treeline and within a few feet intersects with the Crawford Path (Appalachian Trail) to the northeast of the summit of Mt. Eisenhower. The CT actually crosses the A.T. and does not run with it for any length. Instead the CT picks up the junction with the Edmands Path (a few feet up the Mt. Eisenhower Loop) and descends that trail down to Mt. Clinton Road.

But before leaving the heights, climb left (southwest) and ascend the Mt. Eisenhower Loop, which is a direct line to the massive domed summit and the monstrous stone cairn standing on the very top.

Timberline

You are now fully above timberline and completely exposed to the full brunt of the prevailing westerlies. The trek out of the Dry River Valley is well protected as it lies in the lee of the winds. But as you crest the southern Presidential ridgeline, you are hit head-on by the wind. Many days of the year, the velocity of these winds can be ferocious. Climbers approaching from the protected south can hear the impending gale as the atmosphere howls over the ridge on its subsonic way east. It is startling to climb in relative calm up the south flanks of the ridge only to walk straight into the teeth of a hurricane.

The Bernulli Effect

Meteorologists know the reason for "the worst weather in the world" on top of the Presidentials. They call the acceleration of the winds along the great range the Bernulli Effect. This phenomenon is created when a high elevation level of dense air just above the Presidentials caps the rise of westward moving air over the ridge. Because the Presidential Range creates an effective north-south barrier to the west wind, the wind is forced to increase in velocity to move over the heights. This faster moving air is then squeezed between the ridgeline and the dense cap of air above. With nowhere to go, the west wind is pinched between these two physical barriers and accelerates rapidly sometimes to alarming speeds—much the way water in a hose sprays farther and much faster when you pinch off the diameter of the hose itself.

The Bernulli Effect is a principal reason why people die from exposure in the White Mountains—even in summer. A rain squall comes up suddenly and the wind begins to howl over the summits. People in soaking T-shirts and cotton blue jeans can succumb to hypothermia very quickly as the wind and wet act like a very effective high-powered air conditioner.

High Ground (4,761 Feet)

On the summit of Mt. Eisenhower, you are standing at the highest point on the CT. On the southern Presidentials, Eisenhower is king, its view commanding. Mt. Washington's massive summit cone and its structures are clearly visible. The level "lawns" below that summit are all that remain of the "base" uplands that once covered thousands upon thousands of square miles of northern New England. All those ancient uplands have been worn away by 200 million years of unceasing erosion. Only the hardest cores are left standing about, of which Mt. Eisenhower is but one great example.

Below Mt. Washington, Lake of the Clouds Hut seems a stone's throw away. Mt. Jefferson and the other 5,000-foot pinnacle peaks of the northern Presidentials march away to the north.

The Cohos Trail does not venture northward along the A.T. There is so much foot traffic along the north-south ridgeline that the CT need not bring anymore guests to the party. Mt. Eisenhower will do just fine, thank you.

The Arctic

This peak is a massive half-bowling ball dome, with lots of room to roam around on its naked crown. At your feet, tucked between the rocks are arctic plants native to the taiga of northern Labrador. After the ice age glaciers retreated, these cold-loving plants could only survive in the tiny tundra niches remaining after the vast forests returned to reclaim the lands.

You are truly standing in an arctic environment. It can snow on Mt. Eisenhower in July. Snow sticks to the ground for good in early September and can last into late May and even June. In winter, you can not come here unless you are wearing full high-peak assault clothing. Often Mt. Eisenhower simply disappears from sight. Clouds lock up the Presidentials for the majority of the days of the year. Some cloud cover is so thick that it is easy to lose the trail. That's why stone cairns (human-built rock piles) have been erected all over the trail systems above timberline. These little stone clusters loom out of the gloom often enough (in most cases) to keep you on a proper heading. After tarrying on the top, march back down to the intersection where you came and turn left (west) and venture down the Edmands Path.

Edmands Path

There is no better built trail anywhere in the White Mountains. The Edmands Path is a marvel of engineering by one man,

71

J. Rayner Edmands, who in 1909 overhauled an old path up Mt. Eisenhower one year before his death. Edmands proved to be a master trail builder, erecting crib and rock ramps, cutting wide lanes across steep terrain, running easy-to-maneuver switchbacks, and ensuring proper drainage.

Because of his efforts, the trail from Mt. Eisenhower down to the Mt. Clinton Road trail parking lot is still in exceptional condition today, as are his numerous other trails in the northern Presidentials. For a treadway that climbs several thousand vertical feet in a relatively short distance, it is remarkably easy to climb and descend. In the swale on the ridge between Mt. Eisenhower and Mt. Franklin, the Edmands path leaves the Mt. Eisenhower Loop just before the intersection with the Crawford Path and descends westward. Walk the open slabs downward. Unlike the southern side of the mountain that has forest and scrub running almost right to the very ridgeline, the western slopes are scoured by the wind continuously, so timberline begins much lower down the mountain on the windward side.

This means that hikers are exposed to the power of mountain weather for some 10 minutes before reaching treeline. To make things more difficult in bad weather, the ledges can be slick in rain, and dangerous in icy conditions.

The Edmands Path is never steep. Above timberline, the way eases off the height of land on ledges and set stones that were leveraged into place to create a flat grade. At the trees, the path begins a wide sweeping turn to the southwest around the summit formation descending gradually. Views occasionally open out in the gathering woods.

A small stream cuts across the trail in a ledgy area, then the way becomes steeper and passes through a small stone archway, similar to those that one finds occasionally at drive entrances to turn-of-the century summer homes in the region. Soon enter a lengthy section of trail that is built upon heavy stone cribbing which is a hallmark of Edmands' work. The grade is moderate and the trail flat from side to side, and it's in good repair, even to this day.

Even on these steep flanks, Edmands laid out the trail to angle gracefully across the face of the mountain to keep the grades in check. As the base of the peak approaches, the trail gets a bit of wet underfoot as it picks up an old logging track and leaves Edmands' work behind. The skidway runs down along Abenaki brook. Cross the brook and then several other small rivulets before walking out into a recently expanded trail parking lot, situated about half way between the Crawford Depot at the head of Crawford Notch and the Mt. Washington Base Station Road.

To The Ammonoosuc River

Walk downhill out of the lot to Mt. Clinton Road and turn right. Walk this narrow paved road with its dense canopy of trees overhead until the pavement takes a very tight dogleg turn to the right. In the dogleg, look left. There is a large barrier plate just in the woods painted red and white. Turn southwest by the barrier and work slowly downhill on an old grade that was once cut for carriages and then for excursion trains. Drop easily and steadily through deep woods for a mile on the wide track until you begin to hear the pounding of water confined to a rocky bed.

Look right as the forest brightens and dodge down a spur trail to a small bridge. Out on the bridge, peer down into the froth and spray of the Ammonoosuc River as it fights its way through a tumult of large boulders and holes.

Upper Falls

You are standing above Upper Falls, one of the most popular swimming holes in all of northern New Hampshire. Because it rests just below the Base Station Road, lots of people have easy access to this natural feature, and it is often overrun.

But it's hard to resist playing in the water here, particularly in the big cauldron-like kettle hole at the base of the falls. Water, which got its start at Lake of the Clouds thousands of feet above, pounds into the round basin with its sheer sides and spins 'round and 'round before slopping out and running its allotted course. Young people jump off the ledges around the kettle hole for the sheer fun of it. But once in a while someone doesn't come out. Because the kettle hole is perfectly round with vertical deep sides and water enters the pool at an angle, centrifugal force and hydraulic pressure build up. Most of the time, in the summer, the water isn't moving fast enough to cause swimmers problems. But once in a great while after a storm or during a very wet summer, the forces became strong enough to literally pin humans to the rock walls.

What's the equation? A cubic yard of water weighs six tons? Is that it? It doesn't matter. Suffice it to say that great volumes of water periodically slam through the falls, enough so that anyone firmly caught in the raw power of its grip underwater isn't going to be able to surface.

The first man I ever met in Coos County lost his son in the falls. A snorkeler I talked to one wild summer afternoon said he was pinned down deep in the kettle before he thought to try to inch down to the bottom to see if currents there might sweep him out. They did. He was one excited fellow.

No reason to take fright. Just keep out of the falls when its booming and blowing and looks like it could swallow you whole.

Upper Falls in the Ammonoosuc River.

Bretton Woods

Swing back over the bridge and into the woods again and proceed west (right) down the old rail grade and bridle path. The way levels out at it eases into the Ammonoosuc River Valley at Bretton Woods, moves along through moist forest and near a few beaver backwaters before the horizon opens and the Rosebrook Range crosses your view to the south. A cross-country ski trail sign or two pops up, and the way becomes dead flat.

Suddenly its civilization, as the green fairways of the Mountain Washington Hotel resort stretch away and the walls of the famous, huge red-roofed inn rise into the air. Farther south, the ski slopes of Bretton Woods Ski Area swiggle down Mt. Rosebrook to the big base lodge and other structures at the foot of the mountain.

Work your way around the south side of the famous, now year-round hotel, boasting wide promenade porches so popular in the early 1900s, flying flags, flower gardens, and the various trappings of a fine resort. Once on the west side of the hotel, look for several older structures, one a service building on the left and the other an annex to the hotel on the right. These are on the flats. Walk between the buildings and continue on a very short service road out to the Mt. Washington Base Road, or simply walk out the main access drive and spin around for a world-class view of the great white hotel set against the imposing west wall of the entire Presidential Range.

At the Base Station Road, turn left or at Route 302, turn right (southwest) and walk down to the old Maine Central railroad tracks and bridge along Route 302. A small cluster of buildings rises along the tracks at Fabyans. There is a general store here, where you may replenish supplies.

Deception Bypass

No new trails are permitted in the White Mountain National Forest. Because there is no existing trail over big Mt. Deception (although there is an abandoned one high on the summit ridge atop Mt. Deception), you'll want to move west by the Fabyans buildings and away from the Mt. Washington Hotel. The Cohos Trail must be content to bypass the Dartmouth Range peaks and follow Route 302 a quarter mile 20 feet into the grass along the highway.

Fortunately, snowmobile enthusiasts created a somewhat discernible path here about 500 feet west of Fabyans. This parallels the road, crosses a small snowmobile bridge, and then passes over the Old Cherry Mountain Road, a good but narrow Forest Service road on the north side of Route 302. It pokes uphill and slips through a saddle between Mt. Deception and Cherry Mountain only to run out 10 miles later in Jefferson, New Hampshire. Cross the Old Cherry Mountain Road and pick up an old paved route down to a parking area, set up to hold the car loads of people who want to visit a falls to the west.

Lower Falls

Pass by a home and a bar-gate and follow an old railbed on the level until the Ammonoosuc River swings tight to the trail and the layer-cake sedimentary rocks of Lower Falls come into view. Lower Falls is a slip-and-step falls that gradually descends maybe 20 vertical feet over a considerable distance. Water ripples, foams, froths, and rolls down a great collection of little ledges, creating more sound than fury.

This is a popular spot with families with young children, as the lower end of the falls isn't dangerous in "average" water, as is Upper Falls. Cigarette butts everywhere attest to the popularity of the spot.

Return to the trail and walk westward again. The old railbed makes a big swing southward for a good view of Lower Falls upriver and then makes another wide swing westward around a low knob. The trail pinches in toward the highway then opens out into a big paved parking area that is abandoned during the summer but which is often filled in the winter months with the cars and trailers of cross-country ski buffs and snowmobilers.

Cross the lot and walk out to the road at the lot's entrance. Run straight across the road, which has plenty of traffic on it in the summer months, and turn right (west), and follow the Ammonoosuc River right into the lower United States Forest Service campground at Zealand.

Zealand

The little campground at Zealand has a dozen campsites, and Sugarloaf Campground above and to the south has more in two separate plots. Zealand is a staging area for hikes to the Twin

Mt.-Bond complex, Mt. Hale, the Pemigewasset Wilderness, and two of three easy-to-get-to Sugarloaf knobs with their fine views (not to be confused with Sugarloaf in the Nash Stream Forest). Lots of peaks in the east are called Sugarloaf. The name derives from the gum-drop shape of a cloth-wrapped lump of hard raw sugar that folks in the 18th century commonly called by that moniker. That's how sugar was purchased back then, and peaks of that shape often were labeled accordingly.

Zealand derives its name from the country: New Zealand. The area is listed as such on the early maps of the region. Why it was named for a country half a world away is anybody's guess.

Over a century ago, the area was a busy logging camp, at first employing horses to pull heavy log sleds out of the woods and then utilizing powerful but slow Shay locomotives that could climb steeper grades than conventional steamers.

The forests here suffered several major fires, a final catastrophic one in 1903, which lead to landmark early environmental protection legislation.

Zealand marks the end of the first distinct leg of The Cohos Trail. From Notchland to Zealand, you have been traveling roughly west-northwest.

From this point, the trail begins its relentless push north by north-north. The influence of the Presidential Range becomes less and less, and the distinct culture of North Country grows ever stronger.

ଔଔଔ

PART II
Jefferson Dome

Catching the
4:55 at Cherry Pond

Stories from the Back Woods

It's already 12 degrees below—headed for minus 38. A mammoth Canadian high-pressure system looms over head. You could hit the dark, crystal blue sky with a hammer, and it would shatter into a trillion shards of mirrored glass. No clouds. No waves of heat distortion. No wind to stir the air. Just stinging cold. I love it.

It's dusk on the edge of Cherry Pond as I snowshoe atop the many layers of record snowfall in 1969. The great shallow lake low in Audubon's Pondicherry Wildlife Reserve is buried in quieting snow and bathed in deep azure light. The dark shadows of black spruce spear the snow. There's a hulking charcoal upland on the south side topped with a little needle peak. It's Owlshead on the rump of Cherry Mountain.

I'm looking due east across the lake as night draws 'round its cloak, just before the first stars wink on. What I am looking at is impossible. The sun is over the horizon. If I spin around to the west, I can't see the nuclear orb. But to the east there's a photon fire on the mountains there. The Presidential Range is burning a blast-furnace pink—bright enough to make you squint even in the gathering darkness.

From 6,288 feet, from the upper-most pebble atop Mt. Washington, down to 2,500 feet elevation, the great peaks of the range are pulsating with color, in thorough contrast with the dark hues of blues. The vision seems a surrealist's painting. At 2,500 feet there's a hard demarcation line: brilliance above, darkness below. And if you watch very closely long enough, the line advances upward nibbling at the flanks of Adams, Madison, Jefferson, Clay, Washington, and the rest.

The Sound of Silence

My eyes are filled with spectacle but my ears are filled with profound silence. In the intense cold, nothing is moving. Not a rustle. Not a peep. Nothing.

Wait, there is something, the rush of blood in my temples. I can hear my circulatory system on the job.

Then—boom—a muffled explosion, and then another, loud enough to startle any urbanite. Cherry Pond can't help but expand in this cold. The ice in its banks pushes hard against the land. Since the land just won't budge, the pressure sends sharp rifle-shot, rippling cracks hither and yon in the ice under the quieting snow.

I'm smiling. Grinning widely, chilling my teeth until they hurt. The gods are letting me know that the natural world is my happy home and I can't possibly be anything else but be happy in it.

Days They Were, Long Ago...

When I was young and foolish I would come here to look at this—the finest winter sight that can be had in the White Mountains. But I would come here for another reason, as well.

Trains come here. Slow ones. Freights on terribly rickety tracks, maybe once, maybe twice a day. Or at least they once did. And Lord knows I love trains.

The old B&M line freights had to travel at 10 miles per hour at Cherry Pond because the tracks were in such bad shape back then. Since they were so slow, they would come creeping, crawling up on me, if the wind was high and I was engrossed in something else. But the engine would groan, or a metal wheel would squeal against a well-worn rail, or the headlight would catch my eye, and I'd look to see just what tired metal monster had snuck up on me this time.

When it was late and I didn't feel like walking home, I'd wait for the train to hobble by and begin to jog along with the last car. Even then they'd often do without a caboose. As the last car trundled by, I'd reach up a hand, grab the back ladder firmly and swing myself up on rungs easily, and ride away from Cherry Pond and the flaming Presidential Range.

Down I'd go by the Whitefield Airport where a century ago there was once a town called Hazens and the county fairgrounds, too. Down I'd go into the wetlands, in the swamps where the Johns River collects itself for a run at the Connecticut River valley. Down I'd go to Whitefield village to the little rail yard there, under the white town-hall steeple. I'd always get off just before the train yard, in the woods near where the remains of big, concrete boiler stanchions still stand, loitering with not a thing to do.

I'd walk home and it would be dark, for the flames had gone out on the mountains.

CBCBCB

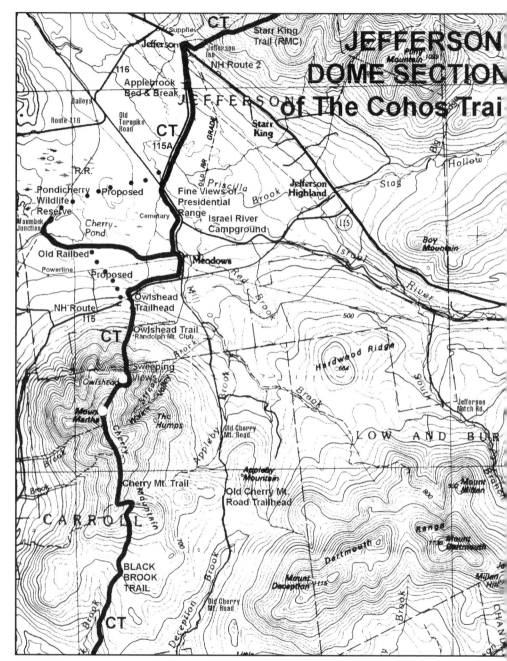

BETWEEN JEFFERSON VILLAGE AND PITTSBURG VILLAGE, A DIS-
TANCE OF NEARLY 90 MILES, THERE ARE NO READILY AVAIL-
ABLE STORES WHERE SUPPLIES CAN BE OBTAINED. TO PLAN
FOR THIS EVENTUALITY, CONTACT WWW.COHOSTRAIL.ORG
FOR INFORMATION ABOUT OUTFITTING FOR THE TRAIL.

The Jefferson Dome

Onward...

With the Presidential Range and Bretton Woods behind you, the second leg of The Cohos Trail is at hand. If you stay overnight at Zealand or Sugarloaf campgrounds, you are a short walk along the Ammonoosuc River away from the unmarked Black Brook Trail, which is the route into first-rate Cherry Mountain and the broad Israel River Valley which sits atop a geological feature called the Jefferson Dome.

Jefferson Dome is a geological term for a rock basement, which holds up other features in a region. The Jefferson Dome is an immense flat granite pluton (magma intrusion) out of which the Dartmouth, Presidential, Crescent, Pliny, and Pilot Ranges extruded 200 million years ago. This dense geological underpinning is filled in with level sediments, which were deposited, for the most part, very recently—during the retreat of the last continental glacier more than 12,000 years ago.

When the Wisconsin ice sheet pulled away from northern New Hampshire, it left great ice and rubble plugs up and down the Connecticut River valley. These plugs backed up what is now known as Lake Hitchcock, a vast inland "great lake" which drowned the valley from Long Island Sound the entire way to where present-day West Stewartstown village sits a few miles south of the Canadian border. Lake Hitchcock spread east and west from the Connecticut River valley where it could and created vast bays, swamping such areas as the Israel River valley that you are about to cross.

I like to imagine what the region was like then, as if I were perched on the bald ledges of Owlshead on Cherry Mountain in the deep past. Instead of flat fertile farmlands below, the whole broad valley would be filled with a vast, rather shallow lake, whose waves would lap at the bases of all the ranges surrounding the valley. The water would be milky in color, from fine flour-like ice-ground silt washing down from the naked mountains so recently relieved of their cloaks of ice.

It would have been a deathly cold land then, and ice would have choked the lake much of the year. Small glaciers would have remained in the Presidential uplands for another few thousand years, carving the U-shaped cirques and valleys that are so familiar to us now.

Lake Hitchcock drained away, reformed and drained away several times in the many centuries after the ice lost its full grip on the land. In some places there is evidence of terraces one atop the other where shorelines once were. As you learn to "read" these pages in the recent geological history of this region of Coos County, it becomes starkly apparent that all the land about us is just so much putty. The land is constantly changing, and in the case of the retreat of the Wisconsin ice sheet, changing very quickly.

In the Jefferson Dome region of the Cohos Trail, you will be walking a good deal in a very young environment, fashioned only in the last thousand decades. And where you will be walking, you will be treading on the heels of paleo-Americans, who, as early as 9,000 years ago, hunted, fished, and harvested wild grains, tubers, and vegetables in the valley.

Black Brook Trail

West of the brown and yellow Zealand Campground sign on Route 302, the Ammonoosuc River broadens out and runs straight to Twin Mountain village. Walk west along the north shore of the river, between it and the highway for 600 feet. A metal retaining wall across the road will disappear behind you, but watch for a gravel tire track running uphill across Route 302. Once you see it, cross directly across the highway to the north. Enter the old road and walk uphill, immediately coming to a gate and a railroad track.

This is the old Black Brook Trail, an old service road that is now officially abandoned and not maintained by the Forest Service. But the old road offers good footing and a pleasant woods walk uphill for several rather effortless miles as it makes for a high junction with the old Cherry Mountain fire-tower road, coming up the mountain from the east. It never crosses the brook that gives the trail its name, as the water course runs well to the west.

The way is obvious, although several spurs cut away and a big sandpit creates a little confusion about 2,000 feet into the climb. At the sandpit, stay to the right along the woods and pick up the trail uphill. The climb out is steady but never tiresome. The path passes a small knob and becomes more gradual for some distance. It then grows steeper as it pulls east of another small knob to rendezvous with the Cherry Mt. Trail.

Cherry Mountain Trail

Turn left at the junction, and leave the Black Brook Trail behind. You are now on the former fire-tower service road known

The Presidential Range on the "floor" of Lake Hitchcock, a vanished glacial lake in Jefferson, NH.

as the Cherry Mountain Trail. The eastern side of the mountain, where you are now, is a portion of the trail that is infrequently climbed. The western section is much more readily accessible, and gets quite a bit of use.

Travel due west for less than a mile, when the trail makes a pronounced turn to the north and begins to run directly upon Cherry Mountain's long north-south ridge. Another old path coming up from the west intersects in the bend in the trail, but stay right on the old service road.

The Cherry Mt. Trail climbs continuously for another mile, but never steeply. It passes yet another old trail on the left before reaching the junction with the western leg of the Cherry Mt. Trail, which enters from the left, as well. Since the development of a parking area just off Route 115 and the placement of a hiking sign, the other trails from the west to Cherry Mountain's high ridges have largely fallen into disuse.

Mt. Martha Summit

Pass the intersection and continue uphill on easy grades for a quarter mile until the forest falls away at a small, level clearing, the former site of the Cherry Mountain fire tower. This clearing marks the first of two of the mountain's well-known summits. It is known by the name Mt. Martha, and is often listed as such on maps of the region.

There are two outlooks here, a little to the left of the summit, both of which are human-made clearings. The first opens out eastward to Mt. Washington and some of the other peaks of the Presidentials. The other presents a rather dramatic view of the major uplands of the Franconia Range, the best view of these peaks that can be had on the CT.

From this angle, Mt. Garfield shows off its pyramid spike well. Massive Mt. Lafayette, the benevolent dictator of the range, displays its rippled, naked summit upthrust, signaling to all that it possesses most-favored mountain status. In your face is North Twin with its slide-scarred face, and its bigger sister, South Twin, which is always hidden from view from virtually every angle in the valleys far below.

Martha's Mile

Cherry Mountain has more surprises, and those who day-hike only to the site of the fire tower, miss the real prize.

Leave the clearing to the northeast and follow a terrific little ridge trail called Martha's Mile for, well, a mile. Upon leaving the clearing, a small cut to the right exposes a view to the east of the Presidentials, but there are better sights ahead.

Martha's Mile is housed in premier spruce and fir forest, keeping the trail cool, moist, and in shadow much of the way. Red needles coat the floor of the trail as it winds downward off Mt. Martha's summit, then undulates along the ridgeline before running up on a jumble of rocks and ledges that take a bit of a scramble to get over.

Once over the bony barrier, you are closing in on a dramatic sub-summit of Cherry Mountain known fondly in these parts as Owlshead. Until recently no trail actually reached Martha's Mile, but in 1999, the Randolph Mountain Club, in a Herculean effort, cut a new and desperately needed bypass to Owlshead, which now slips in to Martha's Mile from the east. This new intersection marks the beginning of the Owlshead Trail, the top of which has been completely relocated.

Pass the new intersection and advance to a set of sensational ledges just under the summit crest, the views from which are nonpareil.

Owlshead

First, a view opens west over the Israel River Valley all the way to Burke Mountain and East Haven Mountain in Vermont. You can pick out strange formations northward too, like crescent moon-shaped Cape Horn near Groveton village 20 miles away, and Goback Mountain, with what looks like a vertical eastern slope that hikers couldn't descend (hence the name, Go Back), in Stratford township 30 miles distant.

There's more. The Pilots, displaying Mt. Hutchins with its exposed granite band-aid on the side, Mt. Mary, and a sliver of 4,180-foot Mt. Cabot, fill in the northwest. The Pliny's, which hide most of Mt. Cabot and Terrace Mountain, stand guard over Jefferson Meadows. Haystack, Starr King, Waumbek, Pliny, and Boy form a great wall to northern excursion. The Crescent Range peaks—Randolph, Crescent, Black Crescent, Sugar, and Jericho—back them up in Randolph Township.

Now for the finale. There are those who say that the view from Owlshead of the western wall of the Presidential Range, the endless Mahoosuc Range, the Dartmouth Range, and Crawford Notch, is the very finest panorama of them all in the White Mountains. The CT isn't a popularity contest, but the view is stunning, breathtaking, or whatever superlative adjective you want to throw at it.

The whole Presidential Range stands out in bold relief. Even Mt. Dartmouth and Mt. Deception close in can't obstruct the vista. And to top it off, like a spy, you can peer down the very maw of Crawford Notch and see hazy blue peaks on the horizon, one of which is actually Chocorua, maybe 35 miles away.

At the opposite northern side of the Presidentials, the great spine of the Mahoosucs undulates like the back of some great saurian beast: Hayes, Cascade, the two Bald Caps, Success, Carlo (the dog), Goose Eye (one of the 10 best in the east), North, Fulling Mill, Mahoosuc Arm, and Old Spec. There is no end to them.

Just above the Owlshead ledges is the true summit. Climb up on the little bump, part the branches of the low growth, and take a peek down into the Pondicherry Wildlife Reserve, managed by the Audubon Society. The big lake and its small neighbor are Cherry Pond and Little Cherry Pond, respectively. You can make out the course of the Vermont & New Hampshire Railroad and the runway of the Whitefield airport, as well as white steeples peeking above trees in Whitefield village.

No one I know can resist Owlshead. Most folks plan to spend a few hours on the heights. I once brought a sleeping bag so that I could witness the world-class sunrise over the "Prezies."

Owlshead Trail

The former route off of Owlshead is now closed, mercifully. The Owlshead Trail has always followed the gully of a massive 18th century landslide. Much of the mountain has long since stabilized, but the steep upper section never did. The soil always remained loose, and hence, eroded easily. The Randolph Mountain Club (RMC), which has long maintained the trail, has wanted to move the upper section for years. In the summer of 1999, they finally received the funding to do the job well.

Retreat from the ledges up Martha's Mile and pick up the new trail coming uphill from the east. The RMC built a long curving, modestly sloped new bypass through cool spruce and fir. It loops around to the north and enters the former trail a bit below the worst of the eroded upper reaches.

The Cherry Mountain Slide

The trail descends rapidly through mature forest and woodlands cut last decade, tracing a course similar to the route of the slide for maybe half its length. In 1885, several days of July rain saturated slopes throughout the mountains. At Owlshead, the upper slopes, sitting atop steep and now thoroughly lubricated bedrock, began to move. The force of thousands of tons of moving rock and soil set off a chain reaction, and some say many millions of tons of mountain came roaring down the valley that day, partially burying a farm and injuring a farmhand, who died four days later.

The slide changed the shape of Cherry Mountain. When the sun is setting in the west, the mountain's north side is illumi-

Owlshead as seen from Route 115A.

nated in slanting sunlight, but the course of the slide there hides in deep shadow. Lit in such a way, it is easy to follow the route the mountainside took on its way to the valley floor.

The Owlshead Trail loses altitude quickly, crossing and following logging tracks, as the pitch becomes less steep. In the lower sections, the RMC has also relocated the trail to relieve a boundary dispute and to avoid some moist areas. It is now well-marked and easier to follow than before.

Two hours from the summit, the trail reaches a small parking area on Route 115. At the head of the lot, the state has erected a green marker, which commemorates the site of the Cherry Mountain slide. In the lot, the view west and northwest is very pleasant. The Jefferson dome, now filled with farms, meadows, boggy forests, swamps, and slow streams, is very evident as it stretches toward the horizon and just this side of flat.

Route 115 And Route 115A

At this time, the CT follows two highways several long miles across the Jefferson Meadows to Jefferson village. In the future, it is hoped that the Cohos Trail Association can procure the rights to place a trail across one of several parcels of private land right alongside Route 115 to gain direct access to Cherry Pond only three-quarters-of-a-mile away. Just 200 feet south of the Owlshead parking lot, a logging road punches west from Route 115 and continues until the land becomes spongy underfoot. It would be a ready-made route to Cherry Pond, but don't take it now.

The public ways will have to do, but they are hardly a disappointment, particularly Route 115A. At the Owlshead trailhead parking lot, cross Route 115 and turn right (northeast). The Pliny and Crescent Ranges are ahead of you and in full view most of the way. Walk a mile to a junction with Route 115A. At the junction, turn left (north), and descend a short distance to the old Jefferson Meadows store, which is now a residence. As you approach the store, an old abandoned Boston & Maine railroad bed crosses the road. Westward (left), down the tired coal-cinder railbed a good long mile, reposes one of the most valuable wildlife environments in New Hampshire, the Pondicherry Wildlife Reserve.

Cherry Pond

If you aren't in a hurry, possess binoculars, and you can sit quietly, Pondicherry Wildlife Reserve is a must. According to the Audubon Society, which manages the lands, more than 60 species of birds call the marshy environment home, from osprey, heron, song birds, seed eaters, to flycatchers, waterfowl of all stripes, bittern, snipe, pileated woodpecker, flicker, and the list goes on and on.

Turn off Route 115A to the west (left) on the railbed. Pass through a new bar-gate and walk out on the elevated right-of-way for 20 minutes. Soon glimpses of water sparkle on your right as the railway approaches Waumbek Junction, once an impossible three-way rail crossing at the southwest end of Cherry Pond.

At the junction, complete with an old switching-box house, keep to the side of the lake, and swing due north along what is now the only active rails left at the junction. Cross a rail bridge over the pond's outlet, and walk north between the tracks and the water, until a broad expanse opens up eastward.

Here you can get a good glimpse of the great expanse of shallow Cherry Pond. And here, reflected in the waters, is the great western wall of the Presidential Range. This is one of the great sights in the mountains and one of the few of the Presidential Range over water. I like to sit down here and stay put for an hour, not moving much at all and not uttering a word. When I first recline, the wildlife seems to have packed their bags and left the place. But every naturalist knows that if you stay quiet long enough, wildlife will resume normal behavior patterns and begin to re-emerge.

You know you have succeeded in your quest for a glimpse of the wild things when you see such tough-to-find creatures as the diminutive green heron or its bigger cousin, the American bittern, its head and beak pointing heavenward and looking for all the world like a big blade of dry grass. And if you are lucky and don't mind slowly fighting your way through alder, beaked hazelnut, and chokecherry, you may uncover the tiny-pet toy of the owl clan, the saw whet.

Cherry Pond and its environs are a moose haunt. Deer frequent the place, otter, muskrat and many other fur-bearers, too. Some will show their faces.

Across the lake, beneath the Whites, a great bundle of sticks tops a dead tree. It is an osprey nest. There are burrows, lodges, well-worn trackways, and otter slides about. Get down on your hands and knees and head into the thickets. There is a lot of life down at the level of a small quadruped.

Dead in Our Tracks

It would be great to be able to wander north along the railroad tracks, out to Route 116 between Whitefield and Jefferson, but the state can't permit access because the rail line is still an active one. By some odd twist of acoustics near the lake, trains can actually sneak up on you if conditions are right. There is no winning a collision with a locomotive. Should the state pull the plug on the rail line (which it owns and leases), The Cohos Trail Association is prepared to request use of the railbed as part of the trail.

Should the trail eventually find a way out to Route 116 and the Turnpike Road, hikers might be able to work their way to the site of a recent dig for Paleo-Indian artifacts. Recent work in the Jefferson Meadows uncovered stone tools, charcoal, and other signs of a camp or seasonal habitation.

Jefferson Meadows

But for now, turn around and retreat back to Route 115A at the old Jefferson Meadows store. At the road, turn left (northwest), and enter the fertile farm fields of Jefferson Meadows. Still to this day, Route 115A is really an agricultural highway running along the edge of great table-flat fields of hay grasses and pasture. Stay left at a junction with another paved road, walk up a little incline, and level out. Pass the Mountain Vale graveyard on the left with its fine iron archway. Mt. Starr King and Mt. Waumbek are over your right shoulder.

The pavement swings right at the junction with the dirt Turnpike Road at the foot of a big dairy barn. Walk directly toward the Pliny Range and cross a bridge over the Israel River. Pause on the bridge and look upstream where cows graze for a look at the Presidential Range stretched out on the horizon. Nothing blocks the view—it's a straight shot right to the foot of the range.

Up the road 1,000 feet, the view is even better in mid-summer, when the hay fields are high with grass. The land here is so flat and broad, it appears as if you are in central Nebraska, and God, for sport, dropped a big mountain range down in the east. With nothing to block the view across the flats, the full vertical scale of the Presidentials is apparent. The range is big, by any standard. Had it been raised up on the foothills of the Flat Irons of Denver's mile-high plateau, the Presidential Range would be considered a formidable mountain mass. If that were the case, Mount Washington would be 12,000 feet high.

Continue north on Route 115A and begin to climb out of the valley. The Waumbek golf course appears on the left, the Jefferson elementary school too, and the charming peach-colored Applebrook Bed & Breakfast with its 24 rooms.

Finally, the road ends at a junction with major east-west Route 2. Right on the corner is a general store, a business where you can stock up for the next big leg in the Cohos Trail. At the junction, if you look eastward (right), you can see a trail sign at the top of a knoll on the left side of the highway. The sign signals the way to the trailhead for the Starr King Trail and the Kilkenny Ridge Trail, both of which are integral parts of the CT.

Jefferson Village

The little hamlet of Jefferson is the last settlement you will enter on the Cohos Trail until you reach Pittsburg, New Hampshire. And even then, if you decide not to cross the big earthen dam at Lake Francis, you can miss Pittsburg village and not enter a "thickly settled" place at all. You can tramp 100 miles to the border without coming across a video store.

Jefferson hosts several large campgrounds within a mile or two, several inns and B&Bs, two or three restaurants, and three active mom-'n'-pop stores. It is a logical spot to recoup, take a shower, buy a hot meal, and take stock of your supplies and physical condition. More than a week of work lies ahead of you, or nearly two weeks if you take your time. Buy some bandages and mole skin for your feet. You'll need it.

CRCRCR

PART III

The Kilkenny

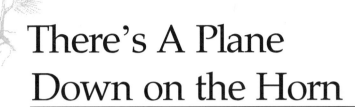

There's A Plane
Down on the Horn

Stories from the Back Woods

In the late '70s, a young couple flying a small Cessna out of Lancaster's grass airstrip ran into a wall of billowing thunderstorms as they headed east toward the Great State of Maine. Finding the going too turbulent, the young fellow piloting the craft banked his plane around and tried to find the airfield again. As he came around, his visibility was cut off by sheets of weather. Guessing now, he headed west-southwest toward Lancaster thinking he had cleared the Pilot Range. He dodged under the clouds to get a visual sighting.

The couple never made it to Lancaster.

The Harsh Reality of Nature

On the north side of Mt. Cabot, a high ridge stretches out which carries a wooded knob, called The Bulge, and the marvelous bald crest of The Horn's pinnacle summit. The Cessna came out of the clouds within yards of the northeast flank of the ridge just a tick and a whistle below the height of land. Everyone wonders what it's like in those last instants before some terrible event when the harsh laws of physics take over the helm and jettison you screaming into the hands of your Maker.

The young man could not correct in time. Sure, he pulled up on the yoke until he bent the damn thing. And he just, just about made it, but the belly of the plane caught the gnarled branches of half-pint, wind-shorn spruce, slowing the flight just enough to ensure a stall. The plane slipped over the ridge, was airborne again for a moment, then belly flopped onto the dense mats of stunted, high-elevation growth. Acting like a shock absorber, the fir and spruce wouldn't let the plane hit the rocks. It skidded and careened along on the branches, sliding, sliding, and sliding some more. By some miracle of fate, the plane never broke up, and came to a gradual halt.

All was quiet. The engine had frozen. The plane's skin creaked and groaned as it settled into its evergreen deathbed.

"You okay?"

"Uh-huh."

"You?"

"Yeah."

The couple took stock of their condition. No cuts, no broken bones. Just a few minor bumps and bruises. Nothing serious. The impact activated the airplane's transponder signal but it went unheard as small craft in the region had all set down to wait out the storm. It wasn't until evening when a lone pilot picked up the distressful beep-beep-beep.

That night the couple had no choice but to rest inside the aluminum skin of the aircraft while the cold of the high mountains seeped into the cabin. They were unaware in the inkwell of night that a crew of rescue volunteers and state officials were amassing at the Mt. Cabot summit cabin after having walked up the Mt. Cabot Trail in the void.

Today, the crew could have walked out to The Horn on the Kilkenny Ridge Trail, but in the early '70s the trail was still a decade away. There could be no advancing at night in the tangle of dense growth along the high ridges. The rescuers reached the plane in the morning, and of course, were struck dumb when two tired, hungry, and very healthy young people greeted them. They could walk. In fact, they could walk out. And they did.

Blessings Untold

I remember the reunion well at the bottom of the trail in east Lancaster. I took a photo of the young woman being embraced by her mother. I'd never seen an embrace like it before or since.

The young woman was alive by some miracle and her mother was clutching that miracle for dear life.

C3C3C3

The Kilkenny

Starr King To Stark

The road to the Mt. Starr King trailhead is only a few hundred feet beyond the last general store (east side of the hamlet) in Jefferson. Cross Route 2 and walk east to the brown trail sign, then turn left uphill on a gravel road that gives access to several private homes. Stay to the left on the road and climb steadily. Before long the trailhead parking lot appears.

Move uphill from the parking lot on the Mt. Starr King Trail along an abandoned road that rises gently and passes an old stone cistern. The trail eventually narrows down, drifts right and becomes steeper in hardwood forest, but the climb is never arduous, as it slabs the western side of the peak. Enter a small opening that supports skunk cabbage, ferns, and trillium in the spring, and jog through several flat sections punctuated with brief climbs.

Fir and spruce begin to crowd in as the trail reaches the 2,800-foot level. About three-fifths of the way along the climb, restricted views open up through to Jefferson and to a western peak off Starr King's shoulder called Mt. Haystack. The trail passes a first-class spring. Stop here and fill your containers. The water is sweet, delicious. The trail then nearly levels off and runs through pleasant woodland with views to the west through the trees.

As the path pushes toward the summit, it becomes steeper

and enters a heavy blowdown area with a young fir understory. Top the ridge to a small opening where the view has grown in. The trees grow no more than 10 feet in height up here as the westerly winds slam into the mountain unimpeded and keep the trees trimmed down.

Mt. Starr King (3,907 Feet)

Trek south on level high ground to a small ledge just beyond the true summit of Starr King. The slab affords the best views of Cherry Mountain, the Jefferson meadows, and several Presidential peaks that the mountains of the Pliny Range have to offer. You can make out big Cherry Pond and Little Cherry Pond, the White Mountains Regional Airport, and Whitefield village. And in the distance the Franconias line the skyline beyond Cherry Mountain and the Dartmouth Range.

Just below the rock slab is a small, grassy lawn at the head of which is a masonry chimney, the only remains of a cabin that once stood here. This is a favorite place to camp, particularly for those traveling north to south. Enough space exists for several small tents.

Mt. Starr King, and King Ravine on nearby Mt. Adams, is named for one of America's great pioneering mountaineers, Thomas Starr King. King was a prominent minister from Boston who tirelessly tramped the mountains before most of the extensive trail system in the White Mountains that we know today was created. But he is best known for authoring *The White Hills*, a book that had great impact on the huddled masses in the cities of New England. Its prose paved the way for an influx of visitors by train and carriage road, and inadvertently spawned a construction boom of large palatial hotels of which only the Mt. Washington and the Balsams Grand Resort Hotel remain.

The good minister was not content to rest from his work in the White Mountains. He eventually settled in San Francisco and did the same thing for the Sierra Nevadas that he had done back east. A summit in that long western range is also named for him.

Mt. Waumbek (4,006 Feet)

The Mt. Starr King Trail leaves the viewing ledge, crosses the little clearing where the chimney stands, skirts the chimney to the right, and slides north into the woods toward 4,006-foot Mt.

99

Waumbek. The trail falls gradually through open, bright woods filled to brimming with ferns in summer. Well below this glade, off the trail and out of sight, is a hideously steep slab of exposed rock that no tree or shrub can gain a foothold on. It is unknown and unclimbed. Approaching it from above is difficult and even dangerous as the mountainside is very steep and there is no ledge to stand on above the near vertical slab.

Continue through the fern glade on the Starr King Trail and within a few minutes the path begins to rise gradually again out of the saddle between Starr King and Mt. Waumbek. It tops out on a flat summit ridge that is overgrown with trees. A small rock cairn marks the summit on Mt. Waumbek. The restricted view to the east is fast closing in as sheltered young spruce put on plenty of growth each year. But you can make out several of the Presidential spires, the town of Randolph, and the foothills of the Crescent Range. The summit cairn marks the end of the Mt. Starr King Trail and the beginning of the Kilkenny Ridge Trail, one of the newest and longest single trails in the White Mountains.

The Kilkenny

Kilkenny is actually an oblique triangle-shaped unincorporated township lying between Lancaster and Jefferson on the west, Stark to the north, and Berlin and Milan on the east. Its name, with a "the" preceding it, has been applied now to the entire region between Route 2 and Route 110. Many miles of trails dissect the region, but it wasn't until the '80s that a through-trail was brushed out that linked some of the more interesting trails into one long right-of-way stretching from Jefferson village to South Pond Recreation Area in the town of Stark.

Now the Pliny Range (Starr King, Waumbek, the multiple summits of Mt. Weeks), the Pilot Range (Terrace Mountain, Mt. Cabot, The Bulge, The Horn—excluding nearby Mt. Mary and the various summits of Mt. Hutchins), and Rogers Ledge have been linked together, allowing a commute across the extensive wooded uplands that make up most of the Kilkenny region. This country is much less heavily trodden than that of the Presidentials and the other ranges to the south because it is less well known, and it is a greater distance from major metropolitan areas. That makes it ideal for experienced trekkers who want to get away from the crowds that frequent the Whites.

If you are going on to points north, please take stock of your supplies. You may need two overnights to complete the journey to South Pond. Do you have enough food with you? Is the skin on your feet holding up well? Are you dry?

The Kilkenny Ridge Trail and The Weeks Peaks

From the summit cairn on Mt. Waumbek, push on northeast two-tenths of a mile to a steep-sided, small knob formation with restricted views over which the trail runs. From this little upland spike, the trail drops to a long level ridge on Waumbek's east flank. The way is flanked with a mossy glade and sweet-smelling low growth for a considerable distance.

The path undulates in cool shade, then drops off the ridge moderately down to a narrow col some 500 feet in elevation below Waumbek's summit, and then climbs quickly nearly 400 vertical feet just to the east of the southern-most side of the three summits of Mt. Weeks (3,884 ft.). An obliterated spur breaks off for the true summit of South Weeks and into a thicket of blowdowns to a summit cairn somewhere in the tangle. In this area there is an unofficial campsite for one small tent.

Pliny and Pilot Ranges from Route 115 in Jefferson, NH.

From the South Weeks elevation, the trail turns sharp right and falls in a series of switchbacks into the col between South and Middle Weeks. A tributary of Garland Brook rests a bit below the path to the left down in the woods, but its source crosses the trail here. There is plentiful, good water in the spring, but the rivulet dries up in the summer months.

The trail up to the middle summit of Mt. Weeks is an easy pull and tops out at 3,684-feet in tight woods with no views. Again the CT falls to a shallow col where there is a sporadic spring and a barely suitable camping spot. The way bears left and begins a moderate uphill push, crosses a small spring, and strives for the highest elevation of the Mt. Weeks trio, the 3,901-foot north peak where the 4,000 Footer Club has established a summit canister. A little spur track runs to a two-person tent site in boreal forest.

Mt. Weeks (3,901 Feet)

Seen from Lancaster village, Mt. Weeks is a perfect bowling ball-shaped peak. In the 1800s, the upland was known as Round Mt., which it assuredly is.

Its present moniker was given in honor of native son, John W. Weeks, whose ground-breaking legislation in Congress, known as the Weeks Act of 1911, cleared the way for the purchase of vast tracts of mountainous and forested lands in northern New Hampshire and Maine—land which had been ravished by indiscriminate logging and hot timber slash fires that destroyed tens of thousands of acres of mountain forest. These federal purchases were the monetary backbone for the eventual formation of the White Mountain National Forest that we know today.

The summit itself offers no views. The boreal fir and spruce have walled off the outside. But the descent northwestward, steep and swinging in switchbacks, turns a bend at one point and the trees part. The narrow opening frames The Horn, a majestic boulder-crested summit that seems close at hand, but in reality, is a full day's hike away.

To Willard Notch and Emergency Walk Out

On the summit of Mt. Weeks, hikers are a long way—at least one full, arduous day—from the Jefferson or South Pond trailheads. The descent from Weeks into Willard Notch and the junction with the York Pond Trail is a time for decision making.

If you or your party are low on food, have sustained an injury, or are suffering extreme discomfort due to excessive cold or heat or black flies, you may want to consider walking out of the Kilkenny once your reach Willard Notch.

The walk off Mt. Weeks to Willard Notch is a long descent, without letup, which passes through open hardwoods, a blowdown clearing, and extensive softwoods on the lower slopes. The descent is reminiscent of the tedious fall off Fulling Mill Mountain to Mahoosuc Notch in the most remote stretch of the splendid Mahoosuc Range that runs 20 and more miles to the east of the CT.

Decision Time

As the softwood forest peters out, the Kilkenny Ridge Trail (KRT) intersects with the York Pond Trail in the heart of Willard Notch. Turn left (southwest) for about 200 feet, then turn right onto the KRT again.

Once in Willard Notch, the York Pond Trail cuts west-east. The shortest route to civilization, should you need it, is a hard left turn and a long pull along Garland Brook to the junction with the Mt. Cabot Trail, then on (keeping left) to Garland Brook Road and Gore Road seven miles outside of Lancaster, New Hampshire. There is a hospital (Weeks Memorial) at Lancaster, and skilled rescue forces, too. There are motels, restaurants, and other amenities, as well.

A hard right turn in Willard Notch on the York Pond Trail leads to a federal fish hatchery at York Pond, about four miles away. Should you or your party be in desperate straits and someone can make it to the hatchery in daylight, help should be available to come to your aid. If the CT is still on your agenda, as it should be, turn left at the junction with York Pond Trail and walk several hundred feet until a hard right turn puts you right back on the Kilkenny Ridge Trail bound for Terrace Mountain and peaks farther north.

The Pilot Range

Once off the York Pond Trail, you are headed up Terrace Mountain and into the second prominent mountain range in the Kilkenny, the Pilot Range. Anchored by 4,000-foot Mt. Cabot, the massive wall that beautifully frames the town of Lancaster stretches from east Lancaster all the way to Groveton village, where it culminates in a fine peak called Mt. Hutchins.

The range hides a lofty northern arm that elevates the summits of The Bulge and The Horn, but this high ground is completely invisible from the villages to the south.

Terrace Mountain (3,665 Feet)

The junction of the Kilkenny Ridge Trail and the York Pond Trail marks the end of the Pliny Range leg and the beginning of the Pilot Range leg of the CT. The Pilots are generally the taller, more exposed and the more interesting of the two ranges that make up the Kilkenny region.

Right away things get more interesting. Terrace Mountain has two summits. Viewed from the west, the peak looks like a double stairstep or terrace, hence the name. But I have a hard time imagining the mountain as a terrace. Better to call the granite bumps by the name Mooseback Mt. or Old Shay, for the stubby Shay logging locomotives that once pounded through the notches on either side of the peak.

But Terrace Mt., it is. A football field length up the Kilkenny Ridge Trail, you'll cross a healthy stream with water in all seasons, then pass a tent site upstream on the left. Enter two separate clearings and ascend gradually for half an hour through fine birch and hardwood forest with terrific views of Mt. Cabot, Bunnell Rock, and Cabot's talus slopes, plus The Horn.

As the trail begins to top out, a spur path to the left leads to the actual summit. This little spur offers excellent outlooks onto Mt. Cabot and Mt. Weeks, with the summit cones of Mt. Jefferson and Mt. Washington fully visible in the distance. At the site of the best vantage point, there is a decent two-person tenting spot.

From the spur trail, return to the Kilkenny Ridge Trail and turn left (west), and soon enter an area that was once a helicopter landing site for, I am told, military maneuvers. It is well grown over, but a little farther on, after passing over a false summit, a second heliport opens up, which is also filling in fast with small softwoods. It's a delightful shady spot in the high country now and offers not a hint of its original purpose.

Nearby is the summit of North Terrace (3,630 feet), which is fully closed in by the cool forest. Descend off the heights on trail that gets progressively rockier and then downright rough as it falls quickly to a second great gap in the mounts, Bunnell Notch.

Bunnell Notch

Much of the way out of Willard Notch and over Terrace Mt., the elevation has increased steadily on the way to much taller peaks. But the deep depression that is Bunnell Notch intervenes, cutting the trekker off from what would otherwise be a cakewalk up Mt. Cabot.

From Terrace's northern summit, the drop is 500 vertical feet into Bunnell Notch. The eastern-most lead of the North Branch of Garland Brook gets its start just off the trail a few hundred feet to the left of the low point in the notch. Water is sometimes available here.

Once in the notch, the Bunnell Notch Trail crosses your path. A signpost lists distances to various points, including half a mile to the Mt. Cabot Trail and 1.9 miles to Mt. Cabot summit, where you are headed. Follow the arrow and the Bunnell Notch Trail a few feet and then swing right, back onto the Kilkenny Ridge Trail.

Toward Mt. Cabot

Climb out of Bunnell Notch easily on grassy terrain rising 300 vertical feet without much effort at all. The Mt. Cabot Trail comes uphill from the south (left). Turn right onto the path. The Kilkenny Ridge and Mt. Cabot Trails run together to the summit now 1.4 miles away.

The Mt. Cabot Trail is a well-used path to the tallest peak in the northern-most and altogether separate public lands of the White Mountain National Forest. Cross a small stream and then enter a section of hardwoods through which you must climb steadily on rocky footing. At a small hardwood clearing the trail turns quickly to the right, climbs steeply, and then flattens out abruptly at an outlook that affords a wide view of the great basin that once held vast glacial Lake Hitchcock where Lancaster village now resides.

Bunnell Rock

With the rush of Bunnell Brook filling your ears, climb quickly up to where a spur trail (someone took the sign) that runs out to

Bunnell Rock, one of a handful of justly famous lunch spots in the White Mountains. Bunnell Rock is a basking rock, a granite ledge just made for humans to lay about like old house cats soaking up the intense solar windfall and the warmth of the rock ledge itself, which has absorbed heat all day if the weather has been fine.

Enjoy the day with a marvelous view of the broad valley below that drains south and southwest to the Connecticut River. The hills to the far west lie in Vermont, to the east are the Pliny peaks, the Carter-Moriahs, and a few Whites. Far away, due south, stands the monolith that is Mt. Lafayette in Franconia Notch, looking like a narrow, ragged-toothed triangle in the sky from this vantage point. In the distant haze to the west, and well south of Lafayette, is Mt. Moosilauke, closer to Dartmouth College in Hanover than it is to Bunnell Rock in Lancaster.

Reluctantly, return to the main trail, and begin a steady climb through a series of switchbacks framed by dense softwoods. Run dead straight for a time until the forest lightens and the trail swings a loop back on itself and wanders up to a small structure with a new front porch—the Mt. Cabot cabin.

Mt. Cabot has a small ledgy crest with fine views as well as a true summit, which is wooded and affords no views. Just below the open crest stands a small wood building maintained by local Boy Scouts, the White Mountains High School outdoor program, and the North Country Trailmaster program. This structure is the former fire warden's cabin. It stands just below where a fire tower once stood. It is the first habitable four-sided structure encountered directly on the CT in the southern stretch of the journey north.

The cabin is a welcome resting and camping spot and a godsend in rough weather for those making the long haul between Jefferson and Stark townships. It is now in good condition, but it was only a few years ago that the United States Forest Service condemned it. It now boasts a good, safe wood stove and a gas range. There is sometimes a cache of food at the cabin that tends to run heavily toward oriental noodles. On the lower floor there is bunk space for eight people. The loft above can accommodate another eight bodies. There is a rain barrel for holding water running off the roof, but the rain catch is missing. Outside a latrine lurks nearby. It is in need of a great deal of work. Scattered about is scrap metal, glass, parts of an old wood stove, and sundry junk. But things are improving; the debris is slowly being removed.

The best thing about the cabin is the sunset from the new front porch. In the quiet of a gentle summer evening, when the wind puffs its last breath for the night, the broad western horizon glows, bathing the peaks with red violet and sending the lowlands into cool cerulean shadow.

Directly behind and above the cabin, a fire tower once stood, the clearing offering a bit more extensive panorama. From here the trail pushes north 2,000 feet to the true summit. The grade is easy and smooth underfoot but the summit is a disappointment for those who have never been up. The forest is dense and the top of the mountain is flat as a griddle.

At the summit, the Mt. Cabot Trail ends, but the Kilkenny Ridge Trail continues north for another 10 more miles. Turn right and enter a whole new realm.

The Great North Woods

The summit of Mt. Cabot marks the demarcation between two distinctly different worlds. South of the summit, the air smells like city money, and the towns begin to bend to the forces of the great American Race de la Rat. North of Cabot, the air smells of money that grows on trees—forest products money. There isn't a McDonald's. There isn't an Office Max. Or a T.J. Maxx. Or Max Factor, or any other Max. That's a fact! Steve Barba, the great white bear of the far north, and one of New Hampshire's most valuable human resources, recognized long ago that the far north, away from the White Mountains, was a distinct region with a peculiar culture all its own. He called the place The Great North Woods.

With his trademark tenacity and connections in the halls of Concord, the state capitol, he convinced Governor Shaheen to proclaim the far north by the very name Steve had been touting all along. And it was done. So when you walk over Mt. Cabot, you enter The Great North Woods, instead of the backwaters of the White Mountains. There is a hint of nobility about it, don't you think? Great North Woods! I like it.

Here paper is king and moose are the guardians of the realm. In mills at Groveton and Berlin, giant paper machines whir at impossible speeds turning out kilos of paper that look a bit like toilet paper rolls but scaled up for something on the order of, say, a King Kong. North of Mt. Cabot, fishing is the national sport of summer and snowmobiling is the national pastime of winter. Hunting is a ritual and a rite of passage. It's something you do. Period. And the folks who live and hunt here know how to use and care for firearms properly.

And, so as not to drag this on too long, the official vehicle of the north is the pickup truck, not the SUV, not the Lexus, not the Camry with the high resale value. The pickup truck. A well-worked one, with its share of dents and scraps, to boot.

The Bulge and The Horn (3,905 Feet)

Leaving the top of Mt. Cabot toward the north, the trekker enters a region where no habitation larger than a few score souls is reached. Except for the towns huddled along the Connecticut River 10 miles to the west—Groveton, Stratford, Colebrook, Stewartstown, and Pittsburg—and the tiny city of Berlin along the Androscoggin River 15 miles to the east (population 13,000 and falling), there are no settlements.

Leave Mt. Cabot on the Kilkenny Ridge Trail through a scrub softwood forest and descend steeply to a shallow saddle in a prominent ridge. Rebound and cross over The Bulge (3,920 ft.), a wooded rounded hump in the middle of the high ridge that ends at The Horn. There are no views from The Bulge.

To the delight of all hikers in this region, the Kilkenny Ridge Trail opened up a route to The Horn, just to the north of The Bulge. This remote summit (3,905 ft.) is one of New Hampshire's unknown and unsung treasures. From either the south or the north, it takes a great deal of effort to reach. Therefore, it isn't frequently climbed. But The Horn has a bald boulder summit that is reached by a short spur path. Coming along the ridge from The Bulge, the spur is ahead and north while the main trail drops off the ridge to the west (left). If you are coming uphill from the north, the spur trail turns left while the main trail moves right.

To get to the very summit, one has to scramble a little with hands and feet to gain the top of the huge summit boulder perched atop a series of other great rocks. From the summit there are exceptional views in every direction, some of the very finest vistas in all of Coos County.

My good friend, Gene Ehlert, and I first came here on the last day of summer. Above 3,300 feet it had snowed the night before. The temperature was just above freezing and the wind velocity was at gale force. The peak is reminiscent of Sugarloaf Mt. well over 20 miles to the north. Both mountains have similar summits with views over remote country that is rarely seen or appreciated.

From The Horn the hiker can look down on Unknown Pond, Kilburn Pond, and the entire Kilkenny region, once laced with narrow-gauge railroad tracks built to haul timber out of the valley. The Presidentials make an appearance to the southeast over the tops of the Plinys. The conspicuous twin Percy Peaks, very long Long Mountain, and Sugarloaf stand out plainly to the north where the CT eventually crosses. The wild Mahoosucs fill in the northeastern horizon, holding up the right-of-way of the Appalachian Trail's most demanding trail section.

To the trained eye, the view north is dramatic evidence of the work of the last great ice sheet that once covered the entire region not much more than 12,000 years ago. It's easy to see the raw wounds that are the south facing cliffs of the Devil's Slide at Stark village and Rogers Ledge far below. Many of the bumps and summits in view have ledgy or spotty south sides too, created when ice pulled southern rock faces off the heights as it bulldozed its way over the heights of land.

Look around. With the exception of the toothpick-size smoke stack in Berlin to the east, there isn't a structure in sight. The vast forests of the Coos spread out in all directions, a sight that is impossible to comprehend when locked inside the mazes of megalopolis a day's drive away.

To Unknown Pond

From The Horn, retrace your steps to the Kilkenny Ridge Trail and begin the descent off the ridge to Unknown Pond 600 vertical feet below, coming down the northern flank of the peak. On the ridge, at the start of the descent, take note of the unusual open softwood forest. I think of it as a sort of cartoon or caricature forest. This is mature, but very short in stature, old growth without much underbrush at the forest floor. It is a rare sight, a botanical treasure in miniature.

The trail descends moderately on a well-laid out course and rounds the long ridge. It runs directly over a small wet area with split-log bog bridges, and then climbs out steeply to the vicinity of the south shores of Unknown Pond. The Unknown Pond Trail stretches across your path. Turn right (northeast) onto it.

Unknown Pond is one of those few remaining unspoiled small bodies of water in New England that give the passerby an understanding of what the eastern continent must have been like before the European settlement. The cold, but shallow lake lies in a depression between two low ridges. The area is carpeted with fern and white birch. It is beautiful.

From the north end of the lake, look across the expanse of water. The Horn stands dramatically above, a towering, yet graceful triangle. The trail runs east just inside the shoreline, then splits, Unknown Pond Trail to the right, the Kilkenny Ridge Trail to the left. At the junction, turn right for now and set up camp in campsites along the trail, or cut left, pass a latrine and several other camp spots, and take a load off or continue northbound.

From the pond, Rogers Ledge is nearly three miles away, and South Pond is more than six and a half miles distant.

To Rogers Ledge

Leave Unknown Pond on the Kilkenny Ridge Trail north, and begin a descent that drops nearly 1,000 vertical feet over several miles. Walk through hardwood forest on a moderate decline until the trail reaches a narrow swamp without trail improvements to help you across the wet area. The way stays level a short distance then pitches down abruptly, opening a wild view of the ragged cliffs of Rogers Ledge in the distance straight ahead.

Following the steep grade, the trail enters the vicinity of Kilburn Pond, a beaver pond and its wetland environs. The path crosses a marsh over five bog bridges that are in very poor condition. Wildflowers abound as you swing alongside little Kilburn Pond, forgotten on most maps. Ramble along the pond on seven bog bridges and re-enter the woodlands on level ground.

You'll reach a set of log steps. Climb them and take a look at Rogers Ledge directly ahead. Cross Mill Brook, a good, year-'round stream and pass the Mill Brook Trail as it enters from the right. In a minute the Mill Brook campsite appears, complete with a latrine and space for three tents. Beyond the campsite, the trail begins a modest climb to the foot of Rogers Ledge cliffs. The trail works right and ascends a long set of well-placed stone stairs to the ledges themselves that stretch high above you. They look raw, weather-ravaged, and imposing.

Rogers Ledge

At the very base of the steep ledges, turn right (east) and climb very steep ground over another stone staircase up to the wooded and flattened summit. A spur trail to the ledges cuts left, while the main trail jogs right. Walk left (south) through a little camp circle and out onto the ledges above the south-facing cliff (that you just hiked beneath) for spectacular views of the wild Kilkenny region.

Numerous trail guides call this viewpoint one of the very finest north of the Whites. The critical acclaim is justly deserved. Few small hillocks anywhere in New Hampshire offer the trekker as much wild real estate to survey as Rogers Ledge. Before you lay the Mahoosucs, the city of Berlin, the Carter-Moriah Range, the Presidentials, Deer and Round Mountains, and The Horn, far above and pinned to the wall of the Pliny Range.

The ledge you are standing atop was once very much a part of a small rounded mountain. The south face was sheered completely away by glacial ice long ago. The forces of such a process are difficult to imagine.

To South Pond

Retreat from the ledges and move north again. Much of the remaining leg of the Kilkenny Ridge Trail is a pleasant and easy woods walk. For a bit over three miles, the trail descends, passes a blue boundary post, picks up old logging roads, and crosses several streams over rocks and bridges. About two hours from Rogers Ledge, the sound of Cold Stream begins to fill the woods. The Kilkenny Ridge Trail passes an old abandoned trail around Mill Mt. on the left. This old way drops southwest down to the village of Stark while the main path continues north to South Pond. The trail is level here and forest duff creates soft footfalls on the earth.

Gradually descend to Cold Brook and cross the log bridge. The remainder of the Kilkenny Ridge Trail runs out another half mile on level ground to South Pond and the federal recreation area there. This is the most direct route north. Wild Indian cucumber grows here.

However, don't continue north just now. Watch for a good spur trail that cuts obliquely left (west) fronted by a sign (on the north side of big a tree) indicating the short pull to the Devil's Hopyard. South Pond is straight ahead. But don't fail to make this turn onto the spur trail and have a rendezvous with the Devil.

The Devil's Hopyard

This is a must see! The Devil's Hopyard is a rare geological formation about half a mile up the spur. It is a small, narrow ice gulch with steep cliff-like sides and a floor crammed with boulders and rocks which have been pried loose from the sheer walls by frost. The formation is akin to the Mahoosuc Notch geology on the Appalachian Trail in western-most Maine and that of Ice Gulch in Randolph, New Hampshire. All were formed by the same forces and share things in common.

The Devil's Hopyard can harbor ice year round, hidden beneath the boulders where a largely unseen stream runs. The rocks are festooned with mosses and fern, which grow well in the cool, moist, shady environment. The mosses make going very slippery in places, and a good deal of effort is needed, and caution is advised. If you are thirsty, the water is cold and excellent to the taste—if you can find it.

The trail runs right through the narrow heart of the Hopyard, rising all the way. At the head of the Hopyard, pass a crumbling cliff, which is being undermined by ice and frost cleaving apart rotted rock. Next week or next century, this cliff face will fall into the narrow valley and seal if off, probably impounding a small pond behind it. After 10 minutes pushing on through the boulder rubble, the trail rounds a low, truly vertical cliff and ends at a new sign urging people not to continue up the steep and fragile terrain at the very rear of the Hopyard. A little more effort to the right on rock boulders and up a steep pitch filled with more great stone, brings you to a tiny cascade, falling from the west wall. In wet weather and in spring, the freshet is delightful. But most of the cascade is invisible, hidden beneath jumble of rocks. You can hear its drumlike-rumble but you can't see the torrent below.

South Pond

Retrace your steps to the Kilkenny Ridge Trail. If bound for South Pond, turn left (north) and walk the lazy path to South Pond and its picnic grounds and small sandy beach. In a few minutes cross a little stream on rock stepping stones and look for a little spur to the right. It goes to a rope swing. Take a dip, but first check the condition of the rope.

Now South Pond's expanse opens up. It is the largest and central body of water in a string of ponds that drain eastward to the Upper Ammonoosuc River. The southern bodies of water are largely undeveloped, but the northern-most one is ringed with camps. This is the South Pond Recreation Area managed by the White Mountains National Forest. Camping is not permitted here, but in rough weather and in a pinch, an overnight in the woods nearby would make good sense.

The recreation area is open all day but closes at night. The access road is gated when the sun goes down in the summer. In the fall—the best time to visit—you can have the place to yourself. Under the stars, the pond steams with summer heat being lost to frosty night air. Canada geese often land here on their way south.

The Kilkenny Ridge Trail ends at the picnic area and beach. Rest rooms huddle in a well-built creosote brown building by the beach. Continue north away from the lake and walk out of the facility on asphalt. Beyond a bar gate some 300 feet, look to your left for an old snowmobile route. Leave the road (90-degrees left) and follow this old trail downhill a quarter mile to a post that is used to support a brown and yellow National Forest sign right along Route 110, a major New Hampshire highway linking Groveton village with the paper city of Berlin.

At Route 110, turn left (west) and walk just a few yards to the Bell Hill Road, which leaves Route 110 to the north, across the highway. Cross the blacktop and enter the Bell Hill Road and its new bridge. Just to the west of the new bridge is the old steel span, a nice place to stop and take in the beauty of the Upper Ammonoosuc River Valley stretching away to the west.

From the bridge the dramatic Percy Peaks stand out against the western sky. Huge, hulking Long Mountain fills in the view to the north. In front of Long Mt. is a modest rounded hump called Bald Mt. Exposed ledges on the south slopes of Bald Mt. are visible through the short growth on the sides of the mountain.

If you look carefully toward the Percy Peaks, you can make out a rounded cone that sometimes seems to get lost in the color of the forest. This formation is Victor Head with its wonderful ledges and sensational view of Christine Lake and the Kilkenny region. The Cohos Trail passes through and over most of this country visible from the bridge.

From the spans, continue north. Cross the railroad tracks and turn left (west) on Percy Road. Walk around a bend and watch for a chain link fence on your left and an orange painted bar-gate on your right. This gate is the entrance to the state's Nash Stream Forest and points north.

Christine Lake in Stark, NH.

Off Trail Feature: Crystal Falls

If you have quite a bit of time and plenty of energy, cross over the tracks and turn right on the old road to the nearly abandoned community of Crystal two miles away. In the village, the road crosses over Phillips Brook, a major Upper Ammonoosuc River tributary. Leave the road left (north) and walk out onto the scoured rock ledges of a low and sprawling stairstep cascade that covers thousands of square feet. In wet weather, this cascade fills up your view and thunders with rushing water, which gathers at the road and virtually roars through a narrow concrete abutment. The first time I saw this I shuddered to think what might happen to an unfortunate soul caught in high water here and thrust through the big square culvert under the road.

Leaving the White Mountains

Once you reach Route 110, the realm of the White Mountains National Forest fades away behind you. Since the first step on the Davis Path, you have been wandering in the White Mountains or in lowlands surrounded by the national forest.

Ahead of you stretches a good deal of new hiking trail and existing ways that have never been used for the purpose of hiking. From here to the Canadian border, The Cohos Trail opens up a lot of new country that no soul but the most intrepid bushwhackers and some loggers have ever seen.

გჳგჳგჳ

PART IV
Nash Stream Forest

The Nash Bog
Dam Disaster

Stories from the Back Woods

Below the naked summit ledge of big Sugarloaf Mountain in the town of Stratford, and threading its way southward through a pristine mountain valley is a stream they call Nash, followed by a gravel road of the same name. Both find their way northward to a depression, which was the 200-acre basin that once held Nash Bog Pond. The beautiful boggy area is full of young-growth forest, sedges, marsh plants, and mosses. It wasn't always that way.

Just Another Day

On a late summer evening in 1969, a Groveton Papers Company employee, who doubled as the Groveton municipal court justice, was driving alone in a blinding rainstorm up the 10-mile Nash Stream Road.

Ralph Rowden was inching along in the torrent on his way to check on a big log and rock-crib dam that held back 200-acre Nash Bog Pond. It had been pouring for two solid days now and he intended to open sluice gates to take the pressure off the old impoundment. But he never made it.

Not far from where the road now crosses a big steel-stringer and wood-plank bridge over the river, Ralph was greeted with a sight from holy hell—and the roar of a thousand black-powder cannons. Nash Bog Dam, built at the turn of the century and under terrible strain, had shattered and collapsed.

A solid wall of water rammed into the forest and began tearing away the trees before Rowden's eyes. The man took the only avenue open to him—he abandoned his vehicle and climbed a

117

tree outside his pickup door just as the waters slammed into the thicket.

There Ralph Rowden stayed the night. All night, soaked and in an unfathomable fright. Oh, the things he must have heard but could not see.

Whole sides of hills were undermined by the flash flood and fell into the valley with a roar. Boulders as large as houses tumbled and cracked against one another as the stream rolled them like dice. Trees everywhere were removed and their bodies whipped, snapped, cracked, and sawed against one another until they were shredded.

And the sound of the flood itself—fluid teeth gnawing at the bones of the land until every morsel of organic material had been stripped away, leaving bedrock, sand, and rounded stones behind.

The Flood Subsides

Some time after midnight, and in tar-pitch darkness, the banshee wail of destruction about him quieted. The lake had drained away.

Now, in the teeming blackness came an apparition. Dancing blue lights began to appear everywhere among the roots of upended trees. All night the cyan fairies danced as phosphorescent microbes, newly exposed to the air, fired off their magical luminescence. Foxfire, it's called.

At first light, Rowden got a look at just how close he had come to having a question and answer session with St. Peter. Piled at the base of the tree he had spent the night in, were the bodies of two dozen trees. They had created a logjam and had rerouted the water enough to keep him from being swept away.

All around Ralph was a moonscape. The whole valley had been scoured raw. Gigantic boulders stood naked unable to clothe their exposed flanks. Landslides had pulled the green carpets off the hills. Thousands of trees had been swept away to jam up under bridges and plug dam spillways in Stark and Groveton.

And Time Passes...

In the cold basement of the Groveton Public Library two years later, after he had fined his last logger for speeding, Ralph, still in his black judge's robe, softly related his night with ill-tempered Neptune.

To his credit, the big man with the boyish face could recall the story with touches of humor. He told me to go up Nash Stream Road and find the tree where he had spent the night. There was a sign posted there, painted by whom he did not know. I had to go, absolutely *had* to go.

I drove up the reopened road the next day and I found the tree and the little sign. It read "Rowden's Roost."

The sign disappeared long ago, but I pine for it, particularly now since Ralph has passed away. I've told myself 50 times that I should go into the garage, slap some paint around, come up with "Rowden's Roost" sign number two, and nail it to the tree. But which tree? Damned if I can remember.

இஇஇ

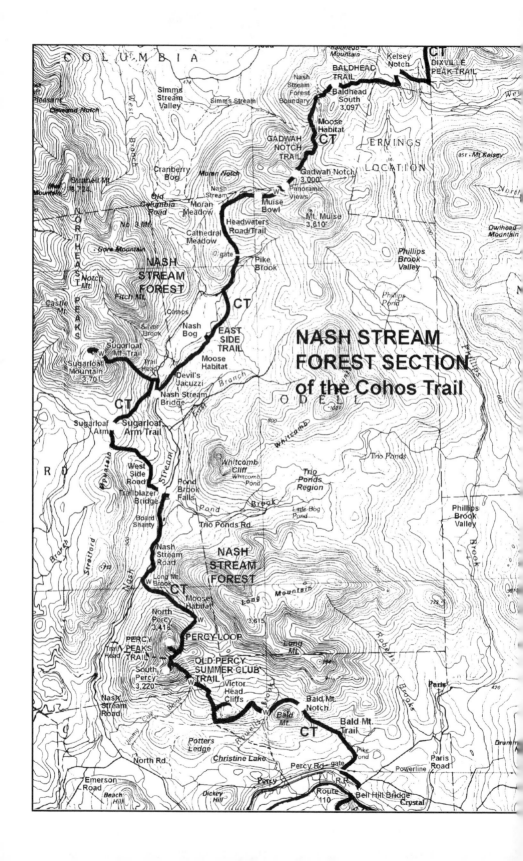

The Nash Stream Forest

The Forest Primeval

Standing at the orange bar-gate on the northern edge of the Percy Road near Percy hamlet a half a mile off NH Route 110, the way northward is through the Nash Stream Forest, a 39,000-acre reserve managed by the state as a multiple-use forest, for recreation, wildlife habitat, and timber.

This great stretch of forest land, with its diverse habitats and outstanding geological features, was once the property of Diamond International Corp. The company sold the land in the late '80s to private interests who were eager to mine gravel and sand from the property.

Numerous conservation organizations and the state of New Hampshire worked feverishly to try to procure the land either for state forest or for additional federal lands tied to the White Mountains National Forest. To the state's credit, New Hampshire officials, together with conservation groups and private and federal appropriations, were able to secure the majority of the property that is now the Nash Stream Forest.

In a very real sense, the Nash Stream Forest is the heart of The Cohos Trail. The property is midway between the southern terminus and the northern terminus of the trail. It is the first great stretch of real estate that is not a part of the White Mountains National Forest, and it is not part of the expanse of private lands to the north that are owned largely by paper manufacturing and timbering firms.

The Nash Stream Forest is home to several lofty summits with splendid views. It harbors a unique ecological rebound area, where the land and its principal drainage are healing itself after the catastrophic Nash Stream Bog disaster of 1969.

There are high elevation spruce and fir forests here that have never been cut and which harbor pine marten, and just maybe, lynx. There are bogs, fens, and small, warm water ponds, waterfalls, high mountain meadows, wild mountain notches, treacherous cliffs, and very steep, dangerous raw granite slabs aplenty.

Around Bald Mountain

The southern entrance to the Nash Stream Forest is the orange bar-gate just off Percy Road (a quarter mile west of the Bell Hill bridge), which continues on to Percy hamlet. This entrance is reached by car by following Route 110 nine miles east from Groveton or 15 miles west from Berlin to Bell Hill Road. Turn north onto the Bell Hill Road, cross the bridge and the railroad tracks. Turn left on the Percy Road and you'll see the orange gate on the right in a minute by car or several minutes on foot.

At the orange bar-gate, walk north through the gate and follow the grassy old road easily uphill under some power lines and through a series of gentle S-turns. The trail soon opens into a small, logged clearing area. Follow it around to the left. Blue blazes show up shortly. Walk by them and in a minute or two, walk past another set of the blue paint swaths on the trees.

Continue westward now, cross a small snowmobile bridge, and begin a lazy uphill grade. Watch the signs and cairns for directions, as several spur trails lead off in various directions. Reach a distinct junction and turn right uphill steeply for a minute, then level out. Climb in open hardwood forest for a mile or so. Soon the hardwoods begin to mix with hemlock and white pine. The trail narrows and becomes a beautiful footpath as the softwoods increase in number and the trail rises more moderately now along the northeast flank of Bald Mountain.

Bald Mountain is a small, isolated hillock that glaciers and fires have played havoc with over the years. On the peak, numerous exposed shelves and ledges peek out to the southeast and northwest. Once in a great while, lightning sets fire to its droughty summit, ensuring that the trees on the heights never get a full chance to completely cover the summit.

As you climb, evidence of severe ice storm damage abounds. Many trees have been topped off, allowing lots of sunlight to reach the forest floor and open up views of the Pilots and Pliny ranges to the south and a look at Bald Mt. itself.

The trail climbs steadily as it approaches a narrow notch between Bald Mt. and a southern ridge of Long Mountain. Walk around a massive log as the trail levels out, then pass through the hemlock-lined little notch with your face directly into the northwest wind.

The trail descends easily out of the saddle and falls into high valley that is a collecting basin for Rowells Brook. Lots of water moves through this area, keeping it moist underfoot in some places. The path slowly hooks around the cliffs on the northwest side of Bald Mt. and runs westward through maturing forest, skirts a wet spot on the right, and slips into a small meadow that is rapidly growing in. Watch for signs and blazes here.

The Upper Ammonoosuc River at Stark, NH.

Bald Mountain and the Percy Peaks are to the west.

Continue downhill on an old Rowells Brook access, an abandoned logging road really, for a short distance. Descend until the trail turns abruptly to cross Rowells Brook, a good source of fast-running water. Cross the brook on a new log and plank bridge built by the North Country Trailmaster youth, and reach the west bank. Descend a few hundred feet on the opposite side of the brook until the trail leaves it for a low ridge. Crest the ridge and move through softwood forest, and then open hardwood until the trail drops into the west branch of Rowells Brook. Hop the narrow stream and pick up yet another abandoned logging track headed downhill. Enter a log staging area that has softened with age and grasses, and drift downhill until the trail turns a tight right and threads west on level ground through pleasant woods on a fairly straight course.

Suddenly the trail opens out onto another pleasant old logging route and turns right onto it. Follow this way northward for a few hundred feet until it ends on a steep eroded grade on the graveled and grassy Jimmy Cole Brook Road.

Turn left, downhill, on eroding slope and follow the Jimmy Cole Brook Road for half a mile—sometimes on level ground, sometimes descending. The road works its way under Victor Head, unseen in the trees on the right.

Watch for a rock cairn about two feet high built on the right side of the trail, which supports a post with a CT sign on it. Turn right (north) and enter the woods. If you turn left, you can walk 1.5 miles out to a public parking area at the swimming beach on the east end of beautiful Christine Lake.

Victor Head Ledge

The CT moves uphill past a huge glacier-erratic boulder and away from the Jimmy Cole Brook Road on what was once known as the Old Percy Summer Club Trail. It heads just west of Victor Head, a low 2,265-foot elevation scarred with bald ledges. A spur trail leaves right in a quarter mile and swings east uphill to the knob with its fine cliffs.

Climb a short, steep pitch on the north side of the knob, move over the height of land, and descend slightly to several flat granite table rocks that drop off straight down. The view is a stirring 180-degree vista, featuring shimmering Christine Lake far below, nestled in expansive forest that is ringed with mountain ranges.

It almost appears as if one could dive into the lake from the ledges, but a jump would fall very far short of its mark.

For a short day trip, there are few better spots in the entire region than Victor Head.

Toward The Percy Peaks

Leave Victor Head on the spur trail and return to the main path. Turn right (north) on the CT and continue uphill on the Old Percy Summer Club Trail onto the southeast flank of the Percy Peaks, two of the most conspicuous mountains in the entire North Country.

Since I first saw them, I have been in love with what look like twin volcanic cores that are known as South Percy Peak (3,220-ft.) and North Percy Peak (3,418-ft.). The perfect rock cones stand side by side, linked by a deep saddle. They are the intensely hard granitic roots of an ancient, long ago-eroded upland plateau. They are fascinating and imposing.

The Percy Peaks are a contrast in extremes. Both have very steep sides with lots of exposed ledges. North Percy is bald on top but harbors a vast expanse of sweet, wild low-bush blueberries that are ripe in early August. South Percy is a gumdrop of a mountain, wooded to its summit but full of steep ledges and crags on its south side and a vast slab on its northeast flank.

The existing hiking trail—the Percy Peaks Trail—ventures up the western side of the mountains. It is short, and until the CT opened, the only recent trail to the summit of North Percy. The Percy Peaks Trail is a moderate and sometimes challenging pull up the peaks. But things weren't always this way. The former West Side Trail, now officially closed, can be dangerous—even deadly.

North Percy is a killer. Two people have died on the mountain, I am told. Both fell—slid, really—to their deaths on the steep but passable exfoliated granite slabs that make up most of the former trail on the west and southwest sides. These slabs often support mosses and lichens which can be as slippery as ice when wet. On the steepest sections, one slip and there is no way to stop the descent. The victims skidded down the rocks and died when they slammed into rocks and trees below.

Several years ago a moose met a similar fate on the mountain, according to North Country resident John Lane. The animal managed to get out onto a steep pitch, slipped and then fell to its death. The unpleasant smell of the huge rotting carcass filled the boreal forest in the vicinity for a good two weeks, according to John.

Old Percy Summer Club Trail

The CT follows the old route of the Percy Summer Club Trail for a while. This historic trail, built perhaps a century ago, is all but obliterated, but its southern end follows a heavily overgrown logging track out beyond Victor Head and toward the vicinity of Jimmy Cole Brook.

Trail has been cleared over the old logging track. It slabs the ridge in mixed forest for half a mile before ending abruptly. New trail turns right uphill and enters a glacier erratic field. These huge blocks of granite, brought here and dropped by the last great ice-age glacier, lay scattered everywhere in the forest, creating a sort of fairyland of odd hulking shapes.

Move through the boulder field and work your way to Jimmy Cole Brook, a reliable source of water. Cross the brook and begin a steady uphill pull toward a wedge between South Percy and an eastern unnamed elevation.

Rising on the southeast side of South Percy, the forest is open much of the way with occasional vistas in the distance through the trees. As the trail approaches the 2,600-foot level, the spruce come on strong and close in around the trail. Soon the CT reaches a granite outcropping that swells in dimension as it rises to the northeast and points directly to the saddle (or col) between South and North Percy. Climb up onto the outcropping, using your hands in some places.

Gain the top and some restricted views open up. On top, turn left (northwest), and walk along the very edge of the granite ledges several hundred feet until they begin to merge with the top of the ridge. Walk over the height of land and descend immediately to the saddle (or col) between the peaks.

South Percy Peak (3,220 Feet)

The CT comes to a T-intersection. This is the South Percy Peak Trail, newly cut from an old bushwhacking path and excessively blazed with gaudy red-orange paint. If you wish to climb

South Percy and its steep and impressive ledges, turn left (south).

Climb the sometimes very steep trail up and over the wooded summit to the many good-sized exposed ledges on the south flank. The view of Christine Lake below, and the Kilkenny wilderness across the valley, is broader and more impressive than from Victor Head.

South Percy is not frequently climbed, as most people want to reach the expansive views from North Percy and the blueberry fields there. Because South Percy tends to be left alone, it is a fine respite from the harried world. You will find few, if any, people here even on major summer weekends.

Take care on South Percy. It is wise to avoid the steepest ledges on the return down the cold north side of South Percy as you make for the saddle and the link to the CT. Be extremely cautious in wet weather and in snow.

North Percy Peak (3,418 Feet)

In the saddle between South and North Percy, turn right (north), uphill. As the CT link meets the Percy Peaks Trail in a few hundred feet, turn right again and climb to the summit of North Percy, passing the new Percy Loop Trail on the right, created as part of the Cohos Trail. Follow the summit trail uphill through scrub and then over steep bare granite slabs punctuated with clumps of low vegetation. On top there are sensational views in every direction without so much as a dozen stunted trees to block the eye.

The summit is expansive. To the west, the old route of the now-closed trail up the slabs drop away at a dizzying angle. To the north, the ledges fall away gently for hundreds of feet and are softened by low scrub. Blueberry plants abound. In early August they are ripe. In September the bushes glow brilliant magenta red.

The hiker is now standing roughly at the center of Coos County and the halfway point of The Cohos Trail.

North Percy (3,418 ft.) gives the hiker a good look at the Nash Stream Forest. The expansive, whale-like mountain to the east is aptly named Long Mountain, its summit a little over 200 feet higher. On Long Mountain's eastern-most uplands is a naked, near-vertical slab—Diamond Ledge. It looks roughly like the state of Texas and is almost never approached except by intrepid mineral buffs.

To the northeast of North Percy are the several summits of Whitcomb Mountain, with its cliff and protected rare plant community. Near the base of Whitcomb, hidden behind Long Mt., are a series of ponds—Trio Ponds, a favorite series of fishing holes. To the north and north-northwest stand the Northeast Peaks, a massive ridge of mountains bristling with wooded summits, the most prominent of which are Sugarloaf (3,701 ft.), with its narrow bald summit ledge, and slightly taller, Bunnell Mountain (Mt. Blue, 2,723 ft.).

The Power of Regeneration

Below Sugarloaf and threading its way south through the valley is Nash Stream, the dirt and graveled Nash Stream Road on the east, and the West Side Road on the west. All point north to a depression that was the 200-acre basin, which once held Nash Bog Pond. In 1969, the big, wood-crib, stone, and earth dam that held back the waters collapsed suddenly during a period of wet weather. The resulting flood stripped the valley of its trees, understory plants, top soil, and even subsoils.

The power of nature to heal is miraculous. From the summit of North Percy, the valley appears green and lush. Nash Stream Forest is fast smoothing out the rough edges under new growth. If you look under the new low brush, however, you can see the raw wounds still.

Some wounds will be slower to heal. Landslides created when the water undermined steep hillsides opened up raw gashes that continue to erode badly, even today. Top soil in some areas was so completely removed that the hardpan earth below is only just now yielding to the tough reindeer mosses and lichens.

But the clear, clean stream runs smartly in its new course, providing nutrients and hydration for the healing process.

The Bowman Valley

Below the summit of North Percy to the east, in the lowlands separating the peak from Long Mountain, is a narrow passage called the Bowman Valley. In maps of the early years of the century, a road once ran through the region. Today, Long Mountain Brook runs northwest paralleled by two long abandoned two-mile logging roads, one to the south and one to the north.

No trail has ever run up the northeast side of North Percy, but the new Cohos Trail now makes it possible to descend in this direction and eventually walk out to Nash Stream Road. In fact, it is now possible to make a circuitous route up, over, and around Percy Peaks from one of two starting points on Nash Stream Road.

Percy Loop Trail

From the summit of North Percy, retrace your steps back toward the saddle between the two peaks. Descend the rock slabs and enter the woods on the trail, but watch to your left. In a few moments a trail breaks left (watch for the CT sign). Turn left and work toward Long Mountain in tight, dark forest on the sunless northeast side of North Percy. This is the new Percy Loop Trail portion of the Cohos Trail.

The path simply rounds North Percy at first, falls and then rises over a fir-locked rise. There you can see terribly steep, exposed ledges on the eastern slopes of Percy. The new footway enters a flat where ice-damaged trees lurk, turns right, and begins to drop through a soil-covered scree field that hides sinkholes among the rocks and small growth. Pace downhill on a modest slope through hemlock, spruce, and hardwoods toward the eastern branch of Long Mountain Brook, which begins below a low col between North Percy and a low rounded knob to the east.

Drop nearly a mile downhill on a modest incline through bands of spruce, birch, mixed hardwood, hemlock, and then birch again until the sound of a small stream begins to fill the woods. The trail sneaks up on the South Branch of Long Mountain Brook and follows the brook downhill until the trail opens out onto the Long Mountain Brook South Road, a tired Class C road that the mountain has fully reclaimed. It has been well brushed out and is easy to follow. Long Mountain Brook rushes and gurgles just ahead down in the valley.

Long Mountain Brook Trail

As the trail enters the aged and leaf litter-filled tote road, look to your right. A small expanse of granite has been exposed by erosion. Water from the stream constantly bathes the rock. It's a cool spot to stop and rest. The water is always delicious here.

Turn away from the granite slab and walk west on the old

track in pleasant terrain for about two miles to the junction with Nash Stream Road. This trail is heavily trafficked by moose. If you encounter one, simply stay calm and make a wide detour around the animal and regain the trail. Moose understand grazing and browsing behavior. If you think a moose is nervous, keep your head and eyes down and pretend to be quietly nibbling the leaves around you. In my experience, this puts the animal at ease, and provides a chance to walk slowly away.

Endless Long Mountain forms the huge wall over your right shoulder as you descend on easy terrain in fine hardwood forest. In late summer and fall, grouse are plentiful in the valley and quite vocal with their calls and ritualistic drumming. The trail here is as pleasant a woods walk as can be had in the whole North Country.

Watch for big beech trees on your right as you drop in elevation. Some carry great numbers of scars from the claws of bears who climb the trees to reach maturing beechnuts. At the base of these trees you can often find small broken limbs, pulled off from the heights by the bears to get at the nuts, then dropped to the forest floor.

As you reach the valley floor, the trail finally comes up along side of fat Long Mountain Brook. The Nash Stream Road is just ahead.

Nash Stream and Pond Brook Falls

For a woods road, Nash Stream Road is frequently traveled. Nash Stream Forest is well managed by the state for multiple uses, but you may never see a logging truck on this road, as timber cutting is scheduled infrequently and in the winter months when the soil is frozen. Instead, the road is popular with local fishermen and women, hunters, a few camp owners, and other outdoorspersons.

The CT and Long Mt. Brook meet the Nash Stream Road at the same spot. Turn right (north) and follow Nash Stream Road with beautiful Nash Stream unseen at first, to your left. Walk 1.8 miles north with the flank of Whitcomb Mountain and the Trio Ponds Road on your right, and Stratford Mountain to your left. Big Sugarloaf looms high ahead. Stay with the stream, following the main road, dodging down an older right-of-way first on your right (after 0.1 of a mile), and then your left (after 0.6 of a mile), for some relief from the dirt road.

A good mile along the Nash Stream Road, the lane to Trio Ponds branches right, uphill. Stay left in the valley and pass rotting "Board Shanty" with its little sign nailed to the siding.

The road narrows a bit and sees a little less traffic now. The forest canopy closes in, and views occasionally open out to pleasant meadows or backwater.

About 4,000 feet beyond Trio Ponds Road, the main thoroughfare crosses a large culvert that channels Pond Brook. Pond Brook drains four small remote ponds called Trio Ponds high behind Whitcomb Mt. They are popular local fishing holes. On the west side of the bridge is a little bowl that makes a great swimming pool. But the big prize is to the east.

**Pond Brook
Falls in Nash
Stream Forest.**

131

Just after you step off the bridge, turn right through a parking spot and walk on a short spur trail into the woods. In only 200 feet the woods open out onto a sensational slide cascade called Pond Brook Falls. The first time I saw Pond Brook Falls, it was during an extremely wet summer. The falls was booming and foaming with power, as water tumbled 200 feet over countless ledges and swept along smooth granite slides. In dry weather, Pond Brook Falls is still a quiet and delightful place to rest. Under the best conditions, the falls is awesome. Either way, it is a must-see spot along the trail.

You can walk up to a tiny outcropping near the top of the falls now on a new trail built by Stratford High School students. There you can view the falls from above and Stratford Mountain to the west.

Trailblazer Bridge

Another 50 feet farther north along Nash Stream Road and the CT cuts west (left) off the road and follows a narrow vehicle track toward the river. A double gate appears. Walk around the one on the left and continue down to Nash Stream. The gate on the right protects a camp. Stay left and shortly reach Trailblazers Bridge, built in 1998 by the Groveton Trailblazers Snowmobile Club and raised higher over the stream in 1999.

This site is where The Cohos Trail Association (TCTA) had planned to build a suspension foot bridge, but the Trailblazers Bridge makes the need for a foot bridge obsolete. The structure is built on donated steel I-beams 90 feet long. The Wausaw Paper Company in Groveton donated the beams, as I understand it.

West Side Road

Cross the well-made structure onto the so-called Stratford Mt. Spur Road, now wide open but once completely filled in with new growth. But stop on the bridge first. The structure offers the hiker a delightful view of a pristine North Country stream. On the western end of the bridge, steep North Percy rears its head to the south, like some monolithic religious icon.

Work your way uphill to a low ridgeline. A small black swamp shows up on the left, filled with a frog chorus of a thousand voices in the spring of the year. Enter a broad, grassy clearing through which the old West Side Road runs. This road comes up from the south from near the main road entrance to the Nash Stream Forest. It is a gated road and sees no traffic.

Turn right (north) on the West Side Road and walk a mile on an undulating roller coaster-like way until the old road reaches a grassy clearing that was once a log yard. Cross the clearing and swing west (left) on level ground toward the Stratford Bog and Goback Mountain region.

At the top of the clearing turn to take a good look at hulking Long Mountain and impossibly shaped North Percy Peak. From this angle its west face looks like the ski-jump outrun hill from hell.

Immediately the trail narrows down to the width of a big bulldozer blade. Heavy equipment use is evident here, as the old trail is opened wide for snowmobiles.

Enter the tighter confines of the trail and stride a quarter mile to a junction. Stay right and immediately begin a long, continuous uphill climb. This ascent rises on Sugarloaf Mountain's southern flank, known locally as Sugarloaf Arm.

Sugarloaf Arm

The path zigzags up the ridge, allowing views out to the south. On the summit of Stratford Mountain behind you, there is plentiful evidence of the severity of the now famous 1998 ice storm. The tops of the trees near the height of land appear to have been raked with shrapnel.

Just when you've had enough of this uphill pull, the trail begins to level out in forest that was harvested about 20 years ago. On your left as you gain the top, big Sugarloaf rears up, its pointy summit showing clearly through the trees and its narrow summit ledge just visible.

The bulldozed ground underfoot on Sugarloaf Arm makes for less than a wild woods experience, but like all other logging paths in these old forests, small plants are already invading quickly. The tracks soften with age and become very pleasant paths indeed.

Roll over the height of land and descend on a steady incline, as steep as the side you just came up on. Cross a new bridge over unreliable water, and walk a good mile through hardwoods out to a junction with the Sugarloaf Mountain Trail, bound for

Sugarloaf's true summit.

Sugarloaf Arm Trail intersects the Sugarloaf Mountain Trail about a quarter mile up the mountain from the trailhead. To climb to Sugarloaf's fine, high ledge for a dramatic 320-degree view of the region, turn left (west) and climb on the steep old fire warden's jeep trail. To descend, turn right (east) and walk out to a weed-filled field that was once a logging yard, the site of a small stream, and a camp. The camp is where the Nash Bog hermit used to hold sway over the free spirits of the valley. The man stayed put summer and winter and led a life of simple self-reliance, a noble style of living that is utterly extinct.

Just beyond the camp is the Nash Stream Road.

Sugarloaf Mt. Trail

A sign on the left side of the Nash Stream Road marks the Sugarloaf Mt. Trail trailhead, about 200 feet north of the second major bridge over Nash Stream.

To get to the trailhead by car, drive east on Route 110 from Groveton about three miles until you see a sign: Emerson Road. Turn left on Emerson Road and motor several more miles until the brown-and-yellow lettered Nash Stream sign comes into view at an elbow turn in the road. Turn left on the gravel Nash Stream Road. Travel about nine miles up the gravel and dirt road until you pass a steel-girder and wood-plank bridge over Nash Stream. Uphill about 200 more feet and on the left is the Sugarloaf Trail sign and trailhead.

Park away from the driveway to a camp, walk up past the camp, and enter the woods on the jeep trail. This jeep trail leads directly and steadily uphill for a bit less than a mile to the site of the old cabin used by the fire warden, who used to oversee the Sugarloaf fire lookout until the mid-'70s.

Once at this site, look for the spring-fed well, just left of the cabin remains, that the warden used as a water source. It is an excellent source of clean water.

The trail continues uphill past the well on a trail that was cut in the '80s around the original route. Follow this uphill to the high elevation and dead level ridge between Sugarloaf and Castle Mountains. Once on the ridgeline, work south (to the left), and walk on level ground out to the narrow rock ledges where the fire lookout cabin (not tower) used to be perched, bolted to the summit.

Sugarloaf Summit (3,701 Feet)

Sugarloaf is fashionable again. In the '70s, the lookout cabin on Sugarloaf's long, narrow summit ledge was removed. It was one of the primary reasons why people climbed the peak back then. Once it was gone, the trail fell largely into disuse and Sugarloaf was relegated to the list of fine summits that people forget about.

But the creation of the Nash Stream Forest helped revive interest in this, one of Coos County's great peaks north of the White Mountains. North of Route 110, it is the highest mountain in the county, save only for Bunnell Mountain (Mt. Blue), the other big bookend of the range that Sugarloaf fronts, the Northeast Peaks.

Sugarloaf has a commanding view of all of Nash Stream Forest, the Phillips Brook Valley summits, the Goback "range" (if you can call it that), Stratford Bog, Mounts Muise, Baldhead, and Dixville. At the edge of the summit ledge, it's as though one is standing on the bow of a ship steering through a blue hillock fastness.

I saw my first moose here. In 1972 the fire watchman pointed to a tiny speck in a small pond west of the mountain but east of Stratford Bog. In the pond were reflections of ripples in all directions and at the center of the ripples was a big, black spot. It was a moose immersed in the water, grazing on water plants for nutrition and sodium.

It wasn't the only creature I met that day though. I waved goodbye to the watchman and headed off the cabin deck and toward the trail when I came up on a porcupine filling the trail entrance into the woods. The quill pig simply stopped and squatted down and turned its left eye toward me. This bristle-bound character wanted to go under the cabin, where the watchman said the big rodent found shelter and had a bedding spot.

It was a standoff, and the porcupine was the one with all the weapons. I sidestepped into the woods and came around behind the animal. It turned its right eye to me, watched for a minute, then shuffled ahead and disappeared under the cabin deck, with nary a mumble or mutter.

To return to the main trail, walk immediately into the woods along the ridge and descend quickly down Sugarloaf's one trail.

A Split Decision

The intersection of the Sugarloaf Arm snowmobile trail coming up from the south and the Sugarloaf Mt. Trail, means it's decision time again. Time to take stock of your supplies, your energy level, and your desire to be alone in the woods for an extended period.

This is a good spot to decide to bail out of the hike if you are not at 100 percent efficiency. Go home.

If you are still up for it, climb Sugarloaf. If not, turn right at the intersection and march downhill to the Nash Stream Main Road and the trailhead of the mountain.

The Route North

Once you are standing at the Sugarloaf Mt. Trail sign and trailhead, you can continue north by turning south (right) downhill. Walk down the Nash Stream Road a hundred feet to the big steel-girder and wood-plank bridge that crosses Nash Stream. Cross the bridge and turn left (north).

The trail follows Nash Stream, Nash Bog flood rubble, and wildflowers upstream. Keep to the east bank of the stream, going north. Watch for yellow blazes painted on rocks at your feet. Go north until you see an old, weed-filled access road break off right uphill. There is a rock cairn built here on your left. Follow this trail to the right uphill and onto leveler ground. Continue north through a meadow filled with raspberry and blackberry bushes (in season), and eventually walk into the woods. The trail rises very gradually on the old road (wet in places in wet weather), until it passes an indistinct height of land at the edge of the woods, then drops a few dozen feet to a grassy flat. The trail swings left abruptly and downhill. At the base of the little ridge, the trail picks up an ancient overgrown way and continues north on level, then gently rising, ground.

Devil's Jacuzzi

Soon the sound of water grows loud in your ears. Look to your left. A little short spur trail launches itself over the bank and a steep dozen feet into a group of overgrown boulders. Run out to a slab in the boiling waters of Nash Stream and have a look around. Directly in front of you as you break out of the woods is a curious natural formation that looks for all the world like a 12-person jacuzzi. The rocks form a true rectangular tub in the stream and capture great quantities of falling water which froths and bubbles—hence the name. (Actually, there is no name for the formation, as it is virtually unknown. I gave it a name in keeping with other formations with a similar moniker in the region: Devil's Hopyard and Devil's Slide.)

Just upstream stand immense boulders. At first glance they look like any other large boulders. But when you examine some of them, you realize that some are composed of different minerals than the surrounding terrain, and some bear what look like recent scars. Indeed, some of the boulders are new arrivals. They were once imbedded in the old Nash Bog Pond dam. When the dam collapsed in 1969, some of the great boulders were rolled into their present position by the titanic currents created as the 200-acre lake drained away.

Take a dip if the water is warm enough and the current is not too swift. High water nearly obliterates the jacuzzi and makes swimming dangerous.

Return to the main trail and turn left (north). The trail undulates easily as it moves up the east side of Nash Bog, located to the west just out of sight in the trees. After a mile, the trail makes a Z-turn, left, then right. By marching straight ahead at the base of the "Z," you can march downhill and out onto the bog.

Beautiful Nash Bog

Here the full extent of a 200-acre wetland opens up, as well as fine views of Sugarloaf Mt., Fitch, Gore, and Castle Mt. ridge too. You can make out a camp or two across the bog. This wetland— once the site of Nash Bog Pond—is home to many bird species, small mammals, and amphibians.

Dodge back into the woods and continue north, skirting the bog the entire way. About a half a mile later, the trail slips out of the woods into a narrow meadow that roughly follows the fully grassed-in old Bog Spur Road north and west. Just before the trail reaches the meadow, another side spur downhill to the bog appears.

On the old Bog Spur Road stay straight ahead and to the left, instead of turning right. Walk the more-or-less level footway pock-marked with moose footprints, droppings, and riotous with wild-flowers for another half mile. Eventually it crosses over a massive iron culvert over Pike Brook with a nice swimming spot below. The trail immediately runs into the gravel Nash Stream Road, now more or less a one-lane road here.

Turn right (north) and walk very gradually uphill by a few camps and alongside Nash Stream's eastern branch, Pike Brook. Pass a demolished school bus, run into the trees here long ago by drunken loggers. Just beyond the bus, the road splits at a camp across from 19-1/2 Road, a rocky, narrow logging track. Stay left on the main way and continue north until an orange bar-gate comes into view. Beyond the gate is the grassy, pleasant Nash Stream Headwaters Road, the gateway to some of the most re-mote country on the entire hike.

This gate can be reached by automobile. Simply continue north on the Nash Stream Road a little more than three miles beyond the Sugarloaf Mt. trailhead. Pass many camps on the west side of the bog, and pass by the first orange gate you see (the Old Co-lumbia Road gate). Continue until you see the second orange gate. Park to the left away from the gate.

Nash Stream Headwaters

Pass around the gate on foot onto the Nash Stream Headwa-ters Road and continue directly ahead uphill. The grassy road climbs gradually at first with running rivulets of water on both sides (in wet weather), and then begins to climb more and more steeply. About half a mile beyond the gate, the trail levels off as it approaches the Moran Notch region and the Columbia town line. Suddenly an expansive open field comes into view, filled with wildflowers and weeds. The field rests on the crest of a broad mountain valley.

The Northeast Peaks

Leave the road-trail and walk into the field—once a logging yard. Depressions in the grasses mark where deer or moose bed down for the night. A terrific view opens up in several directions. I call this field Cathedral Meadow (for whatever reason). I have stood here alone on moody afternoons with the breeze rustling the plants and my ever-more-scarce head hairs. The grand silence of nature steals into the place. You cannot fail to feel a sense of wonder and spiritual ease here. To the southwest and west, lofty dark mountain citadels fill the horizon, Sugarloaf, Castle, Notch, and Gore. To the south, Whitcomb Mountain shows its finest profile. To the north, Number Three Mt. and Bunnell Mt. recede completely into the distant recesses of Columbia Township.

Moran Meadow

Walk out of the field back to the track and turn left (north) again. The path stays level on the plateau for less than half a mile until another meadow begins to come into view straight ahead and the Headwaters Road trail breaks right and uphill.

The meadow before you is sickled down once a year to keep it open so grasses, weeds, and berries fill in instead of trees. In June and July, the meadow is something out of a women's fashion catalog, where mothers and young daughters walk hand in hand, wearing long, peasant skirts and straw hats as they gather flowers.

Off the trail now, if you continue across the meadow due north, you enter the woods on an abandoned trail and find your way to a collapsed log bridge over Nash Stream, which cuts you off from a bushwhacking jaunt to find narrow and secretive Moran Notch and fat little Moran Falls.

Muise Bowl

But the CT turns uphill just before the meadow and climbs steadily along the old road until it begins to ever so slowly level out. On the level now, you enter the enchanted realm of the southwestern flank of Mt. Muise. Before you opens a great natural bowl with high mountain meadows stretching in three directions up to wooded heights.

On the left is a long low ridge that funnels westward through tight Moran notch. This ridge rises and runs on the northwest then relaxes, dipping only 100 feet to a level 3,000-foot plateau that is the edge of Gadwah Notch. As you then gaze north and east, the plateau gives way to a big wooded peak which was given a name only two decades ago. A friend of mine, David Dernbach, calls this natural bowl the Garden of Eden and wildlife heaven. Moose graze here often. Bear turn over logs looking for ants and they pick raspberries and blackberries in late summer. Good clean sources of water flow here and a square mile of new leafy growth, topped off by young spruce and birch, thrust toward the sky. Few people ever come here and no human noise finds its way into the bowl. It's peaceful, so peaceful.

High Mountain Meadows

The Cohos Trail slips across the meadow northward, crossing a deep culvert ditch, and keeping right along the treeline. A skid trail rising on the right becomes evident. Take it. It climbs gradually uphill out of the bowl but soon opens out onto a second meadow that is the remains of a logyard that is not quite fully filled in with grasses and weeds. On the right ahead is a large pile of rotting logs. They were never carted away after a logging job. There is a big skidder tire or two here, as well.

Pass in front of the logs on the level, running through a fertile berry patch, and then descend to Nash Stream.

Nash Stream is a rivulet at this point, but it is the best, most reliable source of water for many miles to come. Fill you water bottles here. Don't fail to do it.

In low water the stream is easy to cross, but in high water after a daylong soaking rain, the little freshet can become wider than you can actually jump across. If the water is raging through this gully and you can't leap over it, do not attempt to walk through it. It will knock you down and sweep you into the woods. It is terribly powerful.

On the other side of the stream, walk uphill now to a raw wound in the soil. This is a bulldozed cut, a staging area for logs that wasn't used much at all. Plants are just beginning to grab a foothold here. Walk across on the very northern edge.

The Great Wall

Stop here, however, and have lunch or a snack. The view is outstanding to the west. All about you is open meadow, created from a logging cut 10 years ago. The elevation is near 3,000 feet, so things grow back slowly up here. Now that the spot is part of the Nash Stream Forest and is above the voluntary no-cut zone of 2,700 feet, this area will slowly revert back to its natural state and support those animals and plants that were once common here.

You have a front row seat to the Northeast Peaks, a great wall of mountains sealing off your view to the west to the Connecticut River valley. Like the Presidential Range stretching before Owlshead's ledges many days hike to the south, the gateway to Gadwah Notch, high on the flanks of Mt. Muise, affords a panoramic view of a vast mountain range that is utterly unknown in New Hampshire. It is as majestic as the Plinys or the Pilots, but not a soul ever sees it. It is one of my favorite of all places in Coos County.

It was here that I had my very finest encounter with a moose. I was resting, leaning back against the upper slope of the bulldozed flat, when a full-grown black bull with his huge rack of antlers well grown in and out of velvet, ambled into the meadow from my left. I cocked my head over to watch this great wonder of nature ease his way southward to a small clump of hardwoods about 50 feet away. And there he set about browsing. I stayed put, my hands cupped behind my head as if I were watching television on a couch. He lunched for half an hour, while I reclined at complete ease. Eventually he drifted south to find another patch of hardwood and I drifted north through Gadwah Notch in a very good mood indeed.

Mt. Muise (3,610 Feet)

Walk across the barren flat toward Mt. Muise, then immediately turn left and follow up and around to the left as the trail makes a little hook-turn and continues north on skidder trail through young spruce and fir. You are now at about 3,000-foot elevation, but the trail only climbs a few dozen more vertical feet.

The big peak here, 3,610-foot Mt. Muise, is named after a fine North Country character—a pipe-smoking, wide-smiling, soft-spoken, former NH Fish and Game officer, Arthur Muise. Everyone likes Arthur, but nobody seems to get his mountain straight. Many maps feature no name for the lone summit. Others call it Whitcomb, although the two Whitcomb summits are a bit of a ways to the south. Muise and Whitcomb are a part of the same upland system, however. Even the state continues to get it wrong. Some management publications of the area list the mountain as Whitcomb. But Muise it is, and Muise it will remain forever. Thanks to Arthur.

To this day there is no trail up Mt. Muise, but there is a summit canister up there for those who just love to hike in super dense spruce and fir just to scrawl their name on a pad. There are no plans to cut a trail either, so the peak may remain forever a wild place.

Walk on the old skid trail until it very plainly forks into a Y. Stay to the left at the Y, and ascend gradually, staying to the right on narrow trail cut to the side of the mud-riddled logging track. In a few hundred feet, watch closely on your right. Soon the tightly packed, young softwood trees part and a newly cut four-foot wide trail runs away at a 90-degree angle. Enter this cut, scissored through a formidable maze of new growth and severe blowdowns.

Before the new section was opened here, this area was a nightmare to pass through. This new cut shimmies through Gadwah Notch itself, which is not a notch in the true sense of the word, but a somewhat wide and rather level depression between two elevations. The trail wiggles through a haunt of tortured trees, twisting and turning, then slowly drifts downward off the height of land and away from the wind-damaged growth in the notch.

Baldhead Ridge

On the north side of Gadwah Notch and Mt. Muise the trail descends gradually in mixed forest, crossing an occasional grown-in skidder path now and then. The trail soon runs due north downhill close to the state's blue-blazed boundary trees, signifying the Nash Stream Forest boundary.

About 3,000 feet below the height of land at Gadwah Notch, the trail turns abruptly east just below a boundary stump and pin onto a fine moose trail. Follow this pathway east to a narrow but lengthy upland meadow, which is a favorite bedding spot and rutting ground for moose. Moose have made and keep open the descent pathway. Their beds are dotted about the clearings, and the shallow wallows they paw out in the ground can be found here and there.

These wallows the males create and urinate in. The females come to these wallows, sniff the scent and sometimes roll in the soil in the wallows. The male is usually close nearby. According to NH Wildlife Biologist, Will Staats, it's the females who choose the males in the moose-mating business, and these wallows play a significant role in the process.

142

After walking the length of a football field on the level, watch for a 90-degree turn to the left. Follow the turn north toward the head of this level region, then soon drift off the ridge westward and begin a descent toward the Simms Stream valley. As the descent gets more and more pronounced, a long-abandoned but once well-built logging road, soon cuts directly across your path.

Simms Stream Valley

Descend to the old logging road and cross it near where the state maintains a blue-blazed boundary line. Descend steadily drawing closer and closer to the boundary. Pick up an old skid track as the trail begins to level out. Turn right, then left on the level to a boundary post and pin heavily covered with paint and survey ribbon. This is the southwest corner of a parcel of land that was recently sold by Champion International Corp. to a conservation association.

Here in this lost corner of the county, I was shadowed by a curious barred owl, who stayed with me for 1,000 feet and glided silently from tree to tree, keeping a steady distance of about 50 feet. The bird of prey kept a constant two eyes on me for half the distance, but after a few minutes it began to turn its attention to any sound in the woods, spinning its head an impossible 280 degrees at will. It would check on me again and again, ruffle all its feathers, and then gaze off. I must have bored the poor creature, because eventually it stopped eyeing me altogether and lifted quietly off for I know not where.

The CT now runs north roughly along the boundary at the edge of a moist, new spruce forest growing in the Simms Stream watershed. Soon the trail slips into a tight spruce and fir tunnel then breaks into a narrow open area, and rises moderately as it enters a grassy logging road with some restricted views of remote country to the west. Run north until the CT waddles up to an immense yellow birch tree, the likes that are rarely seen in the forests these days.

This is a boundary tree with a property-boundary post at the base of it. Because of its strategic location at a property-line junction, this tree was never felled. It's a colossus. Unfortunately, the tree has a weak crotch between two huge leader trunks, and there can be no doubt that the tree will split along this weak point sometime in the near future.

143

Continue a moderate climb northward on the lower south-western flank of Baldhead Mountain. The way is lined with blue blazes, rising through mixed forest, then solid hemlock, and then mixed forest again. In two fifths of a mile, the slope levels out in a tiny grassy clearing at the foot of a small stream. Just across the stream is yet another boundary post.

This post marks the northern-most point that the trail runs through lands that are a part of the Nash Stream Forest. Now, the trail begins an east-northeast jaunt that takes it over Baldhead South, through Kelsey Notch, and over Dixville Peak to Dixville Notch.

෫෫෫

PART V

Dixville Notch

To Sleep
with A Moose

Stories from the Back Woods

The temperature sank with the moon, and the dew point came within reach. Moisture gleamed on every blade of grass. Small rodents worked their pathways under the weeds. No insects visited. The dark was blissfully quiet in the forest near remote Baldhead summit.

I slept well under the Milky Way without a tent, without a care. Someone cleared his throat, but it did not register with my somnolent brain. Then the sound came again. I snorted a snore back into my own throat, and my brain switched on my auditory channels. But I was relaxed. I had heard many a noise in the woods at night over the many years, so my silent soul was not alarmed. The sounds drifted down to me, and they landed like downy thistle seeds settling out of the wind.

There's Something Out There

Crack! Crash! And crack again. These sound waves had the force of thunder rolling just beyond my feet. Nature has armed all her creatures with a hair trigger emergency response mechanism. Mine did not fail me. Something very big was upon me and I had to know NOW what and where it was.

My right hand rammed to the bottom of my pants pocket and produced a tiny flashlight, while my eyes swam in the ink beyond my feet. There I could just barely make out two flat shapes of weak photons but that was it. These shapes were well above me and they were moving toward my feet. *Directly* toward my feet.

I fumbled with the head of the light, pointed it eastward and a flash erupted from it. The beam caught an image that will be

146

burned into my drafty barn of a mind as long as this boy pulls molecules of atmosphere into his lungs.

The image had the flicker of the first silent motion picture ever presented. Black, light, black, light, black. There was a face in the photon flash. No, a snout, a big one. There were two red, wood-fire coals for eyes. Beyond were those two flat shapes, brighter than all the rest. These I saw clearly. Antlers.

An Authentic Moose

Here was a full-scale, 100 percent authentic beast, riding on four cushioned treads that were in full walking stride and headed right down the very center of the pathway I was sleeping in. Here was the tallest four-legged creature of North America and the biggest anywhere on the planet, save a few on the plains of Africa. The Abenaki natives of pre-Revolutionary times had a word for this twig-eater. Moose.

The creature stopped the instant the light plowed into his retina. It had never seen such a burst of light in all its night-time wanderings. This new sensation gave reason to pause. I turned the light out and stayed dead still, breathing from my mouth to mask the rush of wind in and out of my lungs. I was trembling with adrenaline overload.

He made the first move. Barely discerning an antler in the void, I thought he moved to my left, crashed over two sapling evergreens, disappeared for a moment, and stopped. In the cool carbon black of night, my ears filled with the basso rush of air pumping in and out of lungs the size of my whole torso. Oh, this was big screen sound. More than the silent screen flicker in the flashlight pulse, these sound waves hard wired my senses to my brain.

He's moving. Here he comes. On my left now. I popped the light on again, then shut it down instantly. But there he was—I could see all ten million grams of him—in that snap shot. Yes, full grown male. Huge rack. Massive shoulders. Almost black in color except for the pale, gray antlers. And close! Just two lengths of me away. The light froze him again. With more of the clearing behind him, and me lying on the ground zipped into my sleeping bag, I could now see the form of his shoulders and rump against the blazing Milky Way. He was an idling locomotive, with the boiler fully stoked. Steam was issuing from all his cylinders. God, moose breath is loud. Loud, I say. LOUD. Time stopped when the moose stopped on my left. Nothing was happening. This was taking too long. The moose had an unobstructed path to leave. He could march straight ahead and exit the clearing, but he was having none of it. He was fixed to the last tracks he had made. A clammy sense of unease began to seep through my adrenaline armor.

Be Brave and of Good Courage

Time to do something bold. Betting that if two flashes from the light had stopped the moose in mid-stride, perhaps a steady, silent beam might drive him away. Good. Okay. That's a strategy. Yes. Good.

The little nickel-and-dime flashlight launched its beam. I played it directly into the moose's eyes. They beamed back, as red as Francis Scott Key could have possibly imagined. I held the stream of light there, steady as I could, making not so much as a whimper.

Motionless, he was motionless. Geez! Blood in my temples pounded out the seconds.

There. There now. Very slowly, the great beast's mammoth head began to swing away from the direct glare of the light. It was like watching the great door of an Irish castle swing on thousand year-old hinges.

His cranium swung in line with the clearing, and I thought he would move off directly ahead and pass me by. But no. Once the animal had set that huge rack in slow motion, and there was no stopping it.

The head continued to slowly arch away from me. I was transfixed by the deliberate movement. The neck bowed around pulling the clavicle of his left shoulder forward. Now he had to take a step or risk falling over. Yes. A long stride with his left. Then the rump dropped, lowering the center of gravity and coiling the back legs. They sprang back, and the immense creature vaulted off the mark in one bound and was away from me to the north.

I snapped the light off, sat up, and cupped my ears toward the sound of the creature moving off into the woods toward Dixville Peak. A shiver shuddered through me, wringing out every cell in my body. Sleep was impossible for an hour. Every minute noise, a sap droplet on the ground, say, brought a wave of wariness. But the moose was gone. He, nor I, were in a mood for a fight, which is in keeping with both our characters.

Close Encounters of the Moose Kind

When I awoke the morning after the confrontation, early morning fog was draped about the trees and frost-nipped wildflowers. I stood up at the end of my sleeping bag, where my feet had been, and paced off 12 steps—putting heel to toe—to where the moose had first stopped.

Then I turned and paced off the distance to where the moose had stood before he turned and moved away. Another 12 heel-toe paces. Hmmm. The downstairs bathroom is 12 feet in width. He could have stood across the room from me while I brushed my teeth.

Then again, the ceiling is too low in the bathroom to accommodate a moose.

CSCSCS

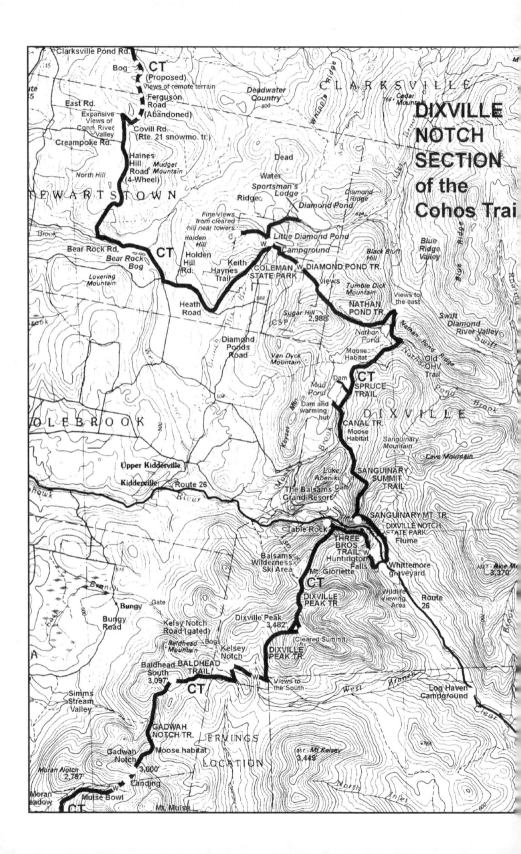

Dixville Notch

Toward Dixville

As you leave Nash Stream Forest, you begin to enter the fifth distinct geographic region of the six that make up the entire length of The Cohos Trail. Just below Baldhead South summit the trail enters the so-called Dixville Notch Region, which extends from this point all the way to Coleman State Park in Stewartstown. The Dixville Notch Region encompasses some of the most dramatic country on the 160-mile journey north.

Baldhead South (3,097 Feet)

At the corner pin deep in Coos forests between Baldhead and Mt. Muise, if you look closely on a birch tree, there is a metal plate pinned to the tree by two bolts. This plate is an old range-line marker of the infamous Van Dyke logging and river-drive firm that dominated North Country timber operations for dozens of years. Old man Van Dyke was one of those tycoons who would have the course of a river changed—as he once did at an oxbow curve in the Connecticut River in Colebrook—to ensure his logs would get to market with less fuss and bother.

At the marker and boundary pin, turn right (east) and follow a small stream in a gully within a short distance of orange-blazed trees designating lands owned by International Paper Company. Climb out of the gully onto a plateau and run east on level ground until the trail meets a moose track. Turn left (northeast) on the moose run and begin an easy climb toward one of two summits of Baldhead South, which reside only 500 feet apart.

Baldhead is a complex of 3,000-foot uplands with four principal elevations. The southern elevation where the CT runs is the tallest. The western and eastern heights are the lowest and the northern one, which is listed on all maps, tops out at just a few feet under 2,700 feet. The northern elevation forms the wall of Kelsey Notch and sports a small bald ledge, hence the name.

The CT swings uphill steeply a few dozen feet and stands on the mountain's highest point, with restricted views through forest that has been severely tested by the western winter winds. Just below and about 500 feet east, however, there is a second elevation, a few feet shorter, which features a fine view to the south and southwest.

Baldhead Viewing Platform

This unknown but pleasing summit is owned by one of the finest gentlemen of the north, Fred Foss. A first-rate engineer, a self-taught forester, and a stalwart conservationist, Foss owns the land on Baldhead South. He is one of the very few people in all of New England who own lands at the 3,000-foot level or above.

Fred continues to purchase big tracts of forest that he wants managed for sustainable and sensible timber harvesting, wildlife conservation, and water quality. He is the very best sort of individual a community or region can harbor, for he will ensure that the lands in his holdings will remain productive, open, and undeveloped.

Now Fred loves his mountain, and he's always wanted to improve the view from the summit of Baldhead South. He has asked The Cohos Trail Association if they would consider building a small observation deck, perhaps 10 to 15 feet high on the summit, so that the eyes of a person standing on the deck would be somewhere between 15 and 20 feet above the forest floor. This modest increase in height would bring into focus a 180-degree panorama.

Baldhead South has a unique perch. From the top the view is directly down the broad, beautiful Phillips Brook valley, with Kelsey Mt. and Owl Head Mt. to the east, and Mt. Muise, Mt. Whitcomb, and Long Mt. to the south. Through this funnel an unrestricted view of the Carter-Moriah Range and much of the northern Presidential Range is visible far away. There are no summits in the way to restrict the view because the Phillips Brook valley opens out onto the Upper Ammonoosuc valley and the major Crescent

Range elevations rise just to one side. So the view is majestic, particularly when you add the heights to the west of Mt. Muise, including the Moran Notch uplands and the northern portions of the Northeast Peaks, anchored by Bunnell Mountain (Blue Mt.).

According to Mr. Foss, there is a secret tucked into the woods nearby, but I have yet to find it. He related that there is a stone or rock slab cave with a very tight opening below the ridge. Through the opening is a chamber, and there is a large pile or formation of grasses and leaves in it. He said he saw it very late in the day many years ago and he could hardly make out the fodder inside. He thought the material had been deliberately arranged by a large animal or perhaps even a human.

To Kelsey Notch

Leave Baldhead South on a high plateau northward, swinging around a devastated area where the winds have leveled most of the trees into a giant game of pickup sticks. Most of the plateau is covered with hemlock and spruce, and the CT threads its way through a maze of blowdowns and dark forests, and around wet

Tom Corridan

A young male moose nibbles on delectable greenery.

153

areas. Eventually the right-of-way begins to decline moderately, passes a tree-filled boggy area, drifts eastward and reaches a steep ravine. Climb down the depression and swing up the other side and around a hummock on the left, and begin a series of drops and levels, that slowly but surely takes you lower in elevation.

Soon the trail enters a chunk of isolated private land owned by Malcolm Washburn of Colebrook, one of the most well-respected loggers in the region. Mr. Washburn was happy to allow the trail to cross his land, but please do not build a fire here or foul the property in any way. Find your way along an ancient logging way in beautiful open forest on a broad plateau. Cross a moose meadow, rise slightly, then pitch downhill moderately and watch for a sharp left turn. Drop down to a small flat open area with a moose trail through it and begin a second steep descent. Level out yet again and cross another moose highway, then tumble off easily downhill, slabbing the lower mountain flanks until the trail bottoms out at the edge of a moist grassy and shrub-filled opening.

The trail keeps to the left of the moisture and begins an easy climb out of the little valley on old logging track. The forest, managed by Mead Corporation and open to the trail corridor through yearly land-use agreements, affords views of Baldhead's flanks behind you, and of Mt. Muise to the south as you rise. This is comfortable going in very isolated country.

Reach a bedrock slab with a yellow marker, and turn eastward for good now. Run out through gently rolling and level country in open hardwood. Even in the summer there are intermittent views to the south across meadows and open forest.

Nearly two miles from the top of Baldhead South, the trail suddenly enters the corridor of what was once long ago a north-south dirt road that connected Phillips Brook country to Kelsey Notch. The road is obliterated just to the south of this intersection, but is easy to follow north.

Turn left (north) at the signpost, and walk the grassy track north a quarter mile to a large clearing at the edge of a broad plateau. This is the head of Kelsey Notch, an area that was once the only way through from Colebrook far to the west to the Androscoggin River valley well to the east.

Kelsey Notch

The trail tips out of the woods at the height of land in Kelsey Notch, a lonely spot that the brisk winds funnel through. Turn 90-degrees right (east bound) and downhill through the notch on narrow, gravelly woods road. The tallest elevation on your left as you descend is one of many arms of Dixville Peak.

As the road bottoms out, it soon crosses a sturdy bridge over a stream draining Kelsey Notch's bogs. Fill your water bottles here if you are desperate for water, but treat the fluid to ensure its safety, particularly in high summer. The bogs upstream are home to lots of small furbearers—bear, moose, a few species of frogs, and many birds. *Giardia lamblia* can fell you within the week if you are careless enough not to take precautions.

Once beyond the bridge, the road becomes a little wider, having seen the sharp blade of a bulldozer more than a few times. In a moment it rises to an intersection. A broad tote road, now a skimobile corridor, cuts left and climbs uphill. This is the Dixville Peak Trail. By moving straight ahead, you'd walk out to the Log Haven Campground in Millsfield some four miles away. Not a bad idea if you're experiencing problems on the trail.

Turn left uphill and begin the long ascent to the summit of Dixville Peak on a trail that has been turned into a snowmobile highway by heavy equipment. This track is popular with riders of the motorized skis, because Dixville Peak's summit has been partially cleared and offers fine views to the northeast, north, east, and southeast in winter, or any time of the year, for that matter.

The bulldozed track makes easy going, but it dampens down the sense that one is in remote country. Such a wide lane seems very much out of place in such an area, but, as with all other such right-of-ways up here, spruce and fir trees will crowd in within the decade and grasses will sprout to soften the hard edges.

Dixville Peak (3,382 Feet)

Dixville Peak is a massive lone sentinel standing in country with virtually no inhabitants. It's wooded all the way to the summit, but the summit has been cleared of scrub a good deal so that views in most directions are afforded from its exposed summit soils.

Climb steadily out of Kelsey Notch on the wide snowmobile trail. You are climbing between one of two of Dixville Peaks six or so arms, which fill up the country south of Dixville Notch. Soon the grade becomes steeper, and fir trees and birch dominate the woods. Eventually the trail crests a ridgeline and follows the ridge north on slightly inclined terrain. The woods to the west have taken a beating here from high winter winds ramming across Colebrook farmlands unimpeded. An hour out of Kelsey Notch, the trail splits to form a summit loop. Stay right and climb uphill a short distance to the top.

From the heights of Dixville Peak, you can see border to border in this narrow corner of New Hampshire, here not more than 30 miles wide. To the east is great, but shallow, Umbagog Lake, with its resident population of bald eagles. To the west is the Connecticut River Valley and its principal trading center, Colebrook. Just beyond the valley is Vermont's Mt. Monadnock, with the Green Mountains in the far distance. To the northeast are myriad low summits of little known peaks filling in the forests of the heavily wooded tracts known as Dix Grant, Dartmouth College Grant, Wentworth Location, plus Atkinson and Gilmanton Academy Grant.

The most immediate peaks in the northeast and north are Rice, Cave, and Sanguinary Mountain, with its dramatic granite sides. The flat-topped summit and ridge to the northwest, with the raw cliff-like granite faces, is Mt. Abeniki, home to the peregrine falcon.

In the far distance to the north, you can make out big Magalloway Mt., the guardian of the Connecticut Lakes. Just to its right is Stub Hill and nearly hidden, farther north, is Rump Mt. just over the border in Maine. Deer Mt. near the U.S. border, pokes up to the west of Magalloway. Even Mt. Hereford in Quebec shows its topknot. At the summit of Dixville Peak, you have entered Tillotson Corp. lands, on which you will stride for the next 12 miles. This venerable Yankee business owns 15,000 acres of well-managed lands, as well as The Balsams Wilderness Ski Resort, The Balsams Grand Resort Hotel, and Tillotson Health Care Company, all of which are located in the Dixville Notch area to the north of the summit, and most of which are heated in winter by a waste sawdust and bark-burning power plant.

The great patriarch of this beautiful domain is Neil Tillotson, one of New Hampshire's towering native sons (actually born just across the Connecticut River at Beecher Falls, Vermont on December 16, 1898) and one of the state's most senior of senior citizens—at 101 years.

In winter, Dixville peak is visited often by snowmobilers, a few of whom tend not to pick up after themselves. Once I found enough trash during a winter visit to fill a jumbo-size garbage bag. (I packed out what I could and a group of responsible snowmobile activists came in and did a fine job of cleaning up the rest.) A flagpole stands near the true summit, complete with tattered American flag, and a heavy iron-cooking grill on the rocks below.

In a quiet snowstorm, Dixville Peak's summit hibernates under the snowflakes, and the place becomes downright peaceful. Snowshoe rabbits work the woodlands everywhere beneath the spruce and fir bows, somehow eking out a living despite winter temperatures that can free fall to 40-degrees-below zero. I've looked for signs of bobcat and lynx that might feed on the plentiful big-footed rabbits, but I've never seen their tracks or scat.

On To Dixville Notch

One of the very best features of The Cohos Trail is now within reach. Leave Dixville Peak on the snowmobile summit trail loop and pick up the main trail in a minute. Head north downhill toward The Balsams Wilderness Ski Resort and the famous and wonderful Balsams Grand Resort Hotel built in 1866 at the head of Dixville Notch. The walk out from Dixville Peak follows the bulldozed snowmobile trail as it cuts S-curves on the ridge, sometimes steeply, sometimes gently. Look underfoot. Sometimes the rock is heavily fractured and is rust-red in color, much different from the granite slabs of Percy Peaks and Sugarloaf now well to the south.

Trek a long mile on the snowmobile trail until it makes a hard dogleg turn to the left and immediately begins a rapid descent to the valley below. Instead of following the wide track left, stay straight ahead and climb on an old narrow woods lane easily uphill for a quarter mile toward the ski area. This narrow trail can be wet in spots. It needs a good bit of work to drain water that is backed up in old ditches and behind forest debris.

Soon the trail opens out onto an alpine ski run. Keep to the right uphill and the anchor tower for The Balsams Wilderness Ski Area chairlift comes into view. Walk along the ridge under the tower and pass the warming and first-aid hut and continue north. On the lip of the ridge that tops the ski area, there are fine views to the west and northwest into Canada. The pyramid in the northwest is Jay Peak near the Canadian border.

If you choose not to visit Dixville Notch, turn left and walk down the ski slopes and down to the parking area a thousand vertical feet below. The Balsams Wilderness base lodge is a beautifully designed structure and is worth a look-see at sometime. If you want to visit some of the grandest terrain along the entire CT (who doesn't?), keep to the ridge top, skirt the ski trails, and walk another solid mile on ridgeline to Mount Gloriette on a good woods trail that is used by cross-country skiers.

Nothing along the trail prepares you for what you will soon see. Within feet of Dixville Notch the way suddenly brightens at a T-junction. The Three Brothers Trail crosses your path. At first, turn left and descend a short steep drop to another trail junction. Coming up from below is the exceedingly steep Table Rock Trail that climbs straight up off Route 26 to the height of land in the shortest possible distance—a near vertical straight line.

Continue left a few feet to a little spur trail to the right. Enter it and suddenly the scrub forest disappears and a naked crag opens up. As you walk out of the woods, the whole world drops away. The forest comes to an abrupt halt and a great chasm opens below you. Dixville Notch.

Dixville Notch and Table Rock

Few places in New England are more dramatic. Dixville Notch appears as if God stabbed down through a mountain ridge with a serrated knife, cutting a narrow, rugged gash between the valleys to the east and west. Unlike all other well-known notches in New Hampshire, Dixville is tightly pinched, short, hideously steep, and filled with frost-shattered spires of rock that reach into the sky. It is more reminiscent of the southwest desert buttes than New England hillocks. Route 26 holds its breath on the way through the divide.

The great rock ledge you are moving out over is Table Rock. It gets narrower and narrower as you approach the edge, sticking out away from the pillar of rock that holds it up below. Finally, at the edge of nothing, the ledge is no more than a few feet wide. The weak of heart have a tough time coming right to the very lip and peering over. There is no better lunch spot in all of New England. If the air is warm and the breeze light, a rarity in these parts, Table Rock is a little slice of heaven. Around you there are spires of dusky red rock and more cliffs. The road is many hundreds of feet below. A recent survey pegged the vertical drop into nearby Lake Gloriette at precisely 701.74 feet.

The view is magnificent east and west, and the rugged cliffs of Sanguinary Mountain are a stone's throw away across the chasm.

Walk over the edge of Table Rock, and it's 700 feet straight down to the road below.

The Three Brothers Trail

Lots of new work has been completed on trails in this region. The North Country Trailmaster program, an association of Great North Woods high school students headed by the able and enthusiastic David Dernbach, has brushed out old abandoned trail and created a whole new path along the heights of Mt. Gloriette, in a successful effort to weave together the more well-known trails in the area into a single, dynamic loop. Turn your back on Table Rock. Walk into the woods and turn left (east) immediately on the new The Three Brothers Trail. Climb the steep pitch and pass the trail you came in on and work eastward.

Just as you begin the pitch uphill, look to your right on the ground. There is a great cleavage here called Ice Cave by the local folks. The rocks appear as if they are slowly pulling apart. Indeed they are. The geology is ever so slowly pushing apart as water gets locked up as a year-round layer of ice under the forest debris and the ice pries the rock apart. Looking at this rift in the rock, it is frightening to imagine the cliff faces in the area separating from the main mountain along this fault line and plunging into valley below in a massive slide sometime in the distant future.

The Three Brothers passes three distinct large cliff and ledge assemblages. At the top of the first one is a tiny outlook toward Table Rock, affording you a look at the formation you were perched on a few minutes earlier.

The trail quickly weaves into the woods and passes a spur trail in 10 minutes that takes you down onto an exposed cliff face that is centered over the very middle of the notch. All this real estate is exciting and deserves at least a day trip if you aren't interested in the entire Cohos Trail.

The only drawback to Dixville Notch is that it is less than two miles long, so it would tend to go by quickly if it weren't for the loop over Sanguinary Mountain, which adds another two miles. Follow the Three Brothers Trail along the south side of the notch in descending woods now until the trail crosses Cascade Brook, enters an ancient logging way, then slips over a low ridge.

Huntington Cascade

With the sound of water filling the woods, the CT grows steep in fine hemlock and swings close to a yawning drop into a deep primordial rock ravine. In the depths, a refined, slender white

160

waterfall leaps from the heights, crashes into a tiny pool, threads through fissures and fractures and a bit lower down the mountain now, cascades over a series of rough rock ledges, foaming and writhing as it goes.

Huntington Cascade is really two falls for the price of one. After a good rain, it can be awesome because its power is so tightly confined to the pinched, tortured ravine. Also, the best vantage points are from above not below the falls, unless you brave the wet rocks and slippery mosses to inch your way into the ravine from below. That's not an easy task and it can even be a dangerous one when the water is high and the falls are thundering and reverberating within the canyon walls.

Dixville Notch State Wayside and Flume

Soon the trail drops away from the falls and fords Cascade Brook. On the other side of the stream the path runs into a cool, tree-filled picnic area managed by the state. Walk down through the picnic tables and out to a clearing next to a salt shed near Route 26. Just across from the salt shed is a tiny graveyard, a touching monument to the very first pioneering family to settle into the cold and forgotten Dixville woods.

This little graveyard tells the tragic story of the Whittemore family who came to the cold frontier to settle a hard-earned piece of land. But within three very difficult winters, the matriarch had perished and her spouse moved westward to Colebrook.

Follow the trail by the little plot, reach Route 26 and cross over it to the trail on the other side. Wander uphill in cool shade to a small parking spot that is the Dixville Notch State Wayside. At the wayside, it is just a short few feet to the base of a flume on Flume Brook. This formation is a rough little gash in the rocks that carries a fat stream of foaming water. It is an infant flume, reminiscent of the great flume in Franconia Notch. It only needs a few million more years of work before it, too, will be one of the great features of the north.

Sanguinary Mountain Trail

Dixville Notch is just too short for a single run through, so now the CT cuts due east along an old, well-established trail along the northern face of Dixville Notch, running along ledges and cliffs on the south shoulder of well-named Sanguinary Mountain

(2,745 ft.).

This low mountain has lots of pleasant surprises. In the fall, usually in the last week of September, the red fall colors of maple leaves and the lowering, slanting rays of the evening sun turn this peak into a brilliant red torch of color—hence the mountain's name. The glow isn't an illusion. The mountain granite is rich in feldspar quartz crystals that reflect light dramatically. At about 7 p.m. for a week or two in the fall, if conditions are right, the mountain is just awesome to behold in its incandescent splendor.

Climb the Sanguinary Mt. Trail steadily, yet easily uphill right along the notch for a good mile, moving in and out of forest, and out onto dramatic ledge. Views of the notch are exceptional most of the way. At the head of the notch, across the chasm from Table Rock, the trail splits in two. The original trail runs downhill sharply and around a bend. A new trail ventures uphill and runs out on a level ridge.

New Sanguinary Summit Trail

Trail crews have built a fine new path on Sanguinary that links the notch to the chain-of-lakes country to the north. In a minute or two a grand vista opens westward from a clearing in the trees at a sharp drop-off. It is a completely unrestricted view to the Connecticut River valley and straight down to the rooftops of the many red rooftops of the European-style Balsams Grand Resort Hotel, a must-stop for presidents, presidential hopefuls, and CT hikers (if you plan to spend the night in luxury).

If you have reservations at the hotel, descend quickly from the outlook to the valley floor and The Balsams via the Sanguinary Ridge Trail.

The Balsams Grand Resort Hotel

This magnificent old hotel far below, one of the very few surviving 19th century grand vacation palaces that graced the North Country, is in the eyes of many, the very best of them all. The location is outstanding, the architecture is New England Victorian, man-made Lake Gloriette is crystal clear, and The Panorama golf course has the finest panoramic view of any course in the entire East. The hotel's Old World feeling and charm is sometimes accentuated by French Canadians who frequent the hotel and who talk rapid-fire Acadian French, a cocky New World version of the mother tongue. N'est pas?

Reservations are required. Visitors are welcome, but a visit in week-old hiking clothes is, well, you understand.

Decision Time Again

For many, The Balsams marks the end of the Cohos Trail journey from the south. Because it is easy to get to and even easier to stay at (if you have more than a few dollars on you), The Balsams is a logical place to terminate the Cohos Trail trek. The hotel marks the end of the high elevation work along the trail and the beginning of a more leisurely trek marked by a host of giant lakes, ponds, streams, and bogs rather than summits. With the exception of the fine open summit of big Magalloway Mountain well off the trail, there are few dramatic outlooks from the heights. However, the great expanses of water reveal a very different and altogether pleasing personality and offer dramatic views all its own.

Now is the time to check your provisions and your mental health. Do you have enough food for at least two more days? If not, you may buy some candy, nuts, and a few basics at The Balsams Staff Canteen, perhaps enough to see you through to Lake Francis. Or you may have to walk three miles west on Route 26 to the Diamond Peaks general store for supplies.

Sanguinary Mountain

The Cohos Trail does not drop down off the ledges to the hotel. Instead, the trail keeps to the summit ridge, rising easily in open woods that afford restricted views, particularly to the east. The new cut moves north of the hotel grounds toward a region of long, little-known ridges and small cold-water ponds.

Trek the new trail along the high country for about a mile, then begin a rather quick descent toward a small mountain sheet of water called Abeniki Pond.

This is all new trail, built by Nathan Richards, a high school student trying successfully to earn an Eagle Scout badge. He, his dad, sister, and some friends, scouted the region, gained permission, and set to work in earnest, creating a fine link between Dixville Notch. It was completed by master trailbuilder, Tracy Rexford, of Lancaster, New Hampshire.

While the trail was being built, Tracy ran into a soccer ball-size nest of hornets. He dropped a hand weedwacker and ran off. I found the tool several days later. Perplexed that someone would leave the tool there, I reached down to pick it up and was stung with the utmost precision right between the eyes.

Abeniki, Mud, and Nathan Ponds

Lake Gloriette, the small pond at the foot of The Balsams, is the first in the series of small lakes that march away to the north and gain in elevation as they go. Gloriette, Abeniki, and Mud Ponds have been built or expanded by people. Nathan Pond is essentially in its natural state.

The first pond above Lake Gloriette is Abeniki Pond, a small charming pool that has been expanded to about half the size of Lake Gloriette. It shimmers beneath Abeniki Mountain's great cliffs and peregrine perches. A service road reaches this pond along Sugar Mountain Brook.

The new Sanguinary Summit Trail tumbles over the high ridge above Abeniki Pond and rushes into the valley, crossing two small log bridges as it goes. It enters an old grassy, tote road, turns right, and runs along Sanguinary's ridge-like form northward in fine forest. The trail eventually bends west to a complex trail junction where numerous cross-country ski trails, a hand-crafted water channel, and an old OHV route jam up against one another in a narrow gap between two low hillocks. Keep to the right through the gap and descend abruptly and turn 90 degrees to the right.

The Canal Trail

The Cohos Trail now rides the unusual Canal Trail, which is the top of a levee that holds back a mile-long, hand-dug canal that brings water from Mud Pond to The Balsams Grand Resort complex. New soil and fill were added to the levee in 1999. The area will be seeded in 2000 to hold the new soil in place.

The Canal Trail slips due north with the black waters rolling alongside. It reaches a crossroads—the Spruce Trail is on the right, Mud Pond is straight ahead. For now continue ahead 500 feet to one of the Great North Woods' most beautiful bodies of water.

Mud Pond was once a natural, shallow pool and wetland. It was originally called Lake of the Floating Islands. But it has been increased in size by the construction of two dams, one at each end of the lake which raised the water level.

The CT wanders up Sugar Hill Brook to a dam. Once on top,

the broad, but shallow, 26-acre lake comes into view, ringed by black spruce and fir. It reposes below the rounded summits of Keysar and Van Dyke Mountains, and is home to loons, waterfowl, and brown trout. Van Dyke (2,778 ft.), is named for the crusty turn-of-the-century timberman who employed hundreds of men in the woods in winter, cutting and then driving logs to market. A small warming hut is nearby to the west. It is operated by The Balsams during the winter months to warm up cross-country skiers.

The Spruce Trail

Instead of swinging along the pond, retreat 500 feet to the trail junction you walked through moments earlier. Turn left uphill, on a dirt and grass track—The Spruce Trail, marked #26—for an easy amble toward Nathan Pond country. Before long, a junction appears on the left that is a short spur down to the northern earthen dam on Mud Pond. A visit to the dam reveals an oddity. Mud Pond drains north here toward the Androscoggin River watershed, while the south dam drains toward the Connecticut River watershed. Few bodies of water anywhere on earth perform such a two-way feat.

Continue up the Spruce Trail to the low height of land and a critical trail intersection. Be sure to take the right turn downhill and through a deteriorating gate that marks the entrance to Mead Corporation lands. As you descend, the trail becomes a muddy track, passes a camp standing off to the left, then swings east and drops into a vast alder thicket crowded into a brooding wetland. The trail threads its way over two snowmobile bridges and right through the heart of the thicket. It is wet underfoot in some places.

Finally the trail tips uphill 10 vertical feet to another critical intersection. Be sure to turn left (northwest) uphill on what is an ancient OHV trail. If you turn south, you could wander for many hours and even days along logging roads that never ever seem to reach a highway.

Walk uphill and over a shallow ridge and fall in deep evergreens to the eastern shoreline of Nathan Pond. There is a metal rowboat here. If you use it, return it exactly to the same spot and be sure to overturn it to keep rain out of it.

Nathan Pond and Blue Ridge

Nathan Pond is near nothing. It is many miles walk in to this cold lost expanse of water. Unlike all the ponds to the south, Nathan Pond has never seen improvements. It is a natural body of water with its original shoreline intact. When you approach from the south, don't linger too long at the shoreline here, because there is a much better observation point on the other side of the lake that is reached in 20 minutes more hiking.

Continue along the east shore trail in dark forest, then mount a low rise and move in a lazy arch eastward in hardwoods. The trail bends almost due east and comes upon a red plastic snow fence. Before the fence, a weedy spur trail abruptly snaps you back north. Take the sharp left turn and pace downhill to the intersection. Turn left at the ledgy rock outcropping, and begin an upward bend which loops up over a low rise now to the west-northwest.

At the height of land, turn around. Behind you to the north and east is a great wall of mountains stretching north-south. In the foreground is the aptly named Blue Ridge which marches north into blue infinity. Behind this upland, you can make out some of the loftier elevations of remote Crystal Mountain, a ridge of indistinct peaks well over 10 miles long. These elevations see the face of woodcutters, but are virtually unexplored by hikers.

Wild Waters

Meander westward now on a board trail pocked with small granite slab patches. Watch for an indistinct spur to the left which takes you back down to Nathan Pond. Approach the pond here and the fine view west over ancient drowned flotsam and stumpage for a good look at lofty Sugar Hill peak (2,998 feet).

When I first came to Nathan Pond, I was greeted by a remarkable site. A flotilla of white snow geese were resting at the center of the black lake. The 50 individuals were almost perfectly spaced apart from one another and arrayed across the pond as if they were an army regiment in dress formation.

The birds, the untouched boreal forest trees around the shoreline, the unearthly quiet, and the remoteness of the place, conspires a sense of wildness of the sort that is now rare in New England.

Nathan Pond is linked by its outflow stream to the Swift Diamond River, and hence to the Androscoggin River and to the gulf of Maine. This cold sink now seals the true character of the last miles of The Cohos Trail. The CT has evolved from a mountainous trek into a wet world—a hike punctuated by open waters, and streams surrounded by countless ridge uplands yet few tall peaks.

Tumble Dick Notch

Leave Nathan Pond for good and run west on the level to a junction and a solid snowmobile bridge over Sugar Hill Brook. Don't cross the bridge, but fill your water bottles. Turn right up-hill away from the span and begin a steady uphill march in broad weed-filled trail toward a distinct gap between Sugar Hill and Tumble Dick Mt. (2,907 feet). With Nathan Pond Brook chattering out of sight in the woods to the right, climb without effort for some distance until the trail narrows a bit and begins to pitch upward in tighter woods. Soon it makes a pronounced S-turn up a steep grade, then tops out at a flat donut-shaped clearing at the head of Tumble Dick Notch. Stay right at the clearing and stride to an opening in the trees. From this spot half a dozen ridge lines snake away into the atmosphere over country few ever visit.

Climb a few hundred feet northward over the notch's height, and begin a gradual descent onto the high Stewartstown plateau and the two Diamond Ponds, the largest bowls of water in the long chain that started at The Balsams now far below.

To Little Diamond Pond

The CT rolls off the heights on an easy grade. The snowmobile path is a "mature" trail that is green, leafy, and pleasant. The woods are quiet and drift by as you descend. At a distinct fork in the way, turn left (west) and soon cross a stream on a well-built snowmobile bridge. Run up the other side and enter a level track that rambles on until it reaches a confusing intersection and almost bends back on itself to the right. Be sure to make the hard turn all the way around the corner here and walk uphill in woods instead of toward Diamond Pond Road or south on the old power line right-of-way.

In a minute, the trail pushes out of the woods and into a small campground with latrines, camping spaces, and two small, rustic structures by the road on the left. As you walk, Little Diamond Pond shows up ahead. Walk down to the shore for a glimpse of a high mountain pond, framed with fir and tucked into low ridge country.

Coleman State Park

You've walked into 1,573-acre Coleman State Park, created in 1957 when the state purchased the estate of Horace C. Coleman to set aside the beautiful high elevation ponds for public use. Little Diamond Pond in the park is the official end of the line for 1999.

For those who have made the long trek nearly 100 miles from the south, there is fresh water, a telephone, and perhaps another body to bump into and chat with. Perhaps! But for the most part, Coleman is deserted. The only people I have ever found at Little Diamond Pond are snowmobilers in winter, who stop for a few minutes on the flats and chat or have a smoke before scooting on over the next hill.

Late one night, while sleeping in the woods at 15 below (two good sleeping bags one tucked inside the another will always do the trick), I heard a herd of young bucks approach Little Diamond, their snowmachines high powered and born to boogie. They whipped across the frozen water and came to a stop in the campground. It was so cold, clear, and still that I could hear their conversation plainly 300 feet away. "Did that guy make it across (the pond)?"

"Who?"

"Don't know. Some other guy?"

"I don't know."

"You see 'em? I don't think he made it."

The young spirits chattered rapidly in the cold about a phantom sled that disappeared on the ice. Soon the voices faded. They did not reach a conclusion. The machines roared to life and the herd rode away from Little Diamond and on toward Colebrook.

"Couldn't be local folks," I thought to myself. "Flatlanders. Massachusetts boys," I convinced myself.

Why did I think such lowly things? Local fellows would have crossed the lake once again. No question. They would have had a look to see if something was wrong, if someone was in trouble. At 15 below, you just do that, that's all. It's one of the fine unwritten laws of the land up here.

Sportman's Lodge and Cabins

On the north side of Little Diamond Pond, a ridge hides a much larger body of water. Big Diamond Pond fills a basin 100 vertical feet below Little Diamond and half a mile farther north.

To reach Big Diamond, walk along the access road, around the west and north side of Little Diamond. Stay to the right at an intersection with a logging road, and work your way eastward on the flank of a ridge above the lake. Soon a rustic lodge comes into view down a steep drive.

On the south shore of this time-honored fishing spot, stands Sportman's Lodge and Cabins. Sportman's is one of a handful of old, authentic hunting and fishing camps that still grace the remote waters of New Hampshire and Maine. Bring a few bucks along with you and you can put on the feedbag, take a hot shower (you'll need it by now), and sleep in a bed to the quiet trill of insects and frogs calling where jet-plane engine and freeway fury doesn't intrude.

Linda and Lee Spector, who own the Lodge, have agreed with the Cohos Trail Association to act as a hiker hostel on the CT system. They will be open for business for hikers in the summer of 2000 at rates conducive to trail vagabonds.

Lost High Country

The Diamond Ponds rest high on an upland plateau. It is not a spectacular feature, but as you will see if you work your way north on the proposed CT or simply motor out of Coleman State Park to Route 26 and southward, the high ground here reveals sweeping vistas because the land is still farmlands, hay lots, or scrub pasture growing in with trees.

The country is not unlike the rolling-hill farmlands of central Vermont or the Catskill counties of New York state, all of which are tied together with narrow dirt farm lanes bordered with old, barbed-wire fencing.

At many a turn, blue 3,000-foot peaks fill in the horizons, standing out against the yellow grasses of late summer and early autumn. From the highlands, you can swing your eyes in an unbroken line east to Dixville Notch, over Dixville Peak, south to Baldhead, Mt. Muise and the Moran hills, southwest to Cranberry Bog Notch, the many Northeast Peaks, Cleveland Notch and Cree Notch, and west to Vermont's Mt. Monadnock.

Unless you get up this high on the Stewartstown plateau, this country will remain invisible. It's invisible now. Barely a soul ever sees it or knows the summits and notches by name.

C3C3C3

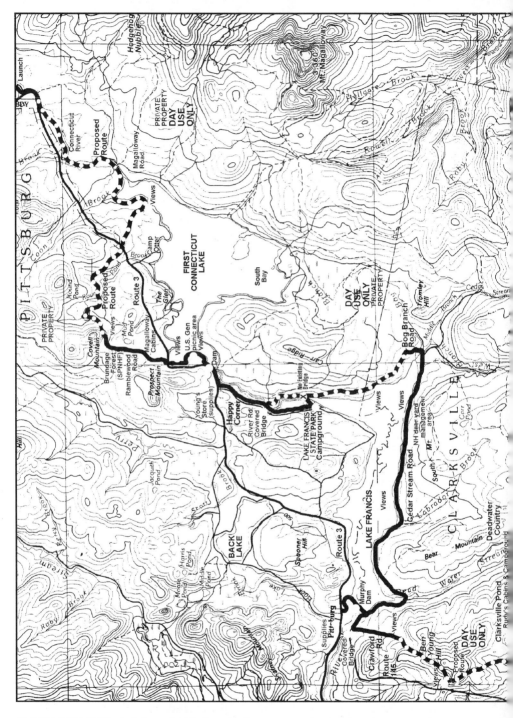

ROTATE THE BOOK CLOCKWISE 90 DEGREES TO PROPERLY VIEW
THE MAP ON ITS NORTH/SOUTH AXIS.

Map continued on page 175.

PART VI
Connecticut Lakes

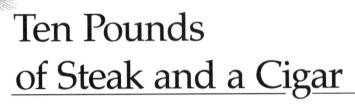

Ten Pounds of Steak and a Cigar

Stories from the Back Woods

John had been eaten alive by black flies. Their venom had done its job, and the poor man lay ill with fever and chills. He didn't want his supper. Not that there was any supper to be had. Bing had promised that Carl would bring dinner that evening, but now it was nightfall and there wasn't a calorie in sight.

Beneath the black church-spire fir trees, we had settled down in Bing's old fishing camp to wait. It was the only camp on Scott Bog, a cold sheet of water by the boundary mountains separating us from Canada. It was late May, and it was still frosty, come evening, this far north.

Famous Pittsburg... New Hampshire?

Pittsburg, New Hampshire, that's where we were hunkered down. It's a famous place, truly famous. There are lots of reasons why. Here are 10 good ones.

1. It's the snowmobile capital of the world. Even has snowmobile traffic jams.

2. It can stake a legitimate claim to being the first place in the United States to secede from the Union.

3. At 300,000 acres, it's the largest town in area in the entire contiguous United States.

4. Most of it is owned by one company that cuts trees but doesn't build Pizza Huts, Tire Palaces, or T-shirt shops.

5. It possesses a drowned village. Honest!

6. It's a pretty good place to smuggle contraband—cigarettes, mostly—in and out of Canada.

7. It could have been the site of twin nuclear reactors (one of which never was built) which now reside at Seabrook, New Hampshire.

8. It's the moose capital of the world, where people go "moosin'" every evening.

9. It's the headwaters of the Connecticut River, New England's biggest, and it shelters a majestic string of cold deep lakes, each one much larger than the next.

10. It has more black flies per capita than anywhere else on planet earth.

Old friend Gene and I had been paddling a canoe around all day, exploring back bays, inlets, and channels. Now we were hungry. But John wasn't, still. He was asleep.

So with a kerosene lamp glowing, Bing, Gene, and I sat around the empty wood-slab table and talked about life among the black flies. And we were having ourselves one of those backcountry male conversations that sets a spouse's eyes rolling around in the sockets, when there came a crunch and crash and an expletive nondeleted.

Damn, if it wasn't Carl slamming through the forest at night without a flashlight.

Bing opened the door to peer out, but before he could throw it back, a big bear of a man in brown conservation-officer-khakis rolled through the portal carrying a big sack with him.

Dinner! Salutations. Greets. How the hell are ya? That out of the way, Carl put the sack on the table and reached in. Out came a package of cigars. Back to the bag. He grabbed and strained and pulled. Out came a steak, a mammoth slab of beef. It was bloody and thick and you could just taste it. Mmmm. Then he reached into the bag again and yanked out a fifth of whiskey.

Bon Appetit

That was it. He crumpled up the bag, put it in the wood stove, threw in some kindling, and lit a fire. We were going to eat steak. Nothing but steak. And we were going to wash it down with whiskey. Nothing but whiskey. And when we were done were we going to smoke cigars. Nothing illegal. And when we were finished we were going to be Men...with heart conditions.

Look, I know this sounds like I'm stretching the truth here. Not one bit. I'm a man of my word. And I'll tell you, the steak was fantastic. The whiskey, well, there wasn't enough of it. The cigars were from the local grocery store, but you don't crave Havana stogies when you're deep in the fir forests of northern New Hampshire anyway. Somehow a White Owl works here, and always will.

John slept through it. The rest of us sat around the table and the kerosene lamp and talked and joked and wheezed into the night.

Like good carnivores, we relaxed in like company and digested the big lump of protein and fat in our bellies. Then we retired and slept like death and snored too loudly.

08080B

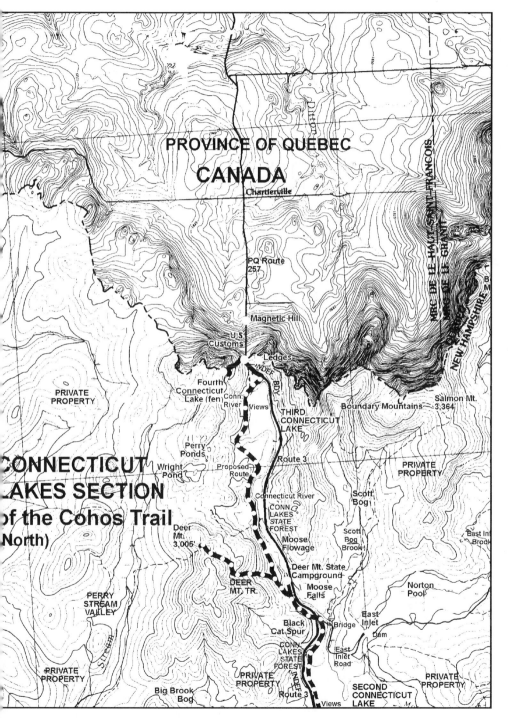

NORTHERN TERMINUS OF THE COHOS TRAIL

Connecticut Lakes

IMPORTANT!

The Cohos Trail north of Coleman State Park in Stewartstown, New Hampshire is in the planning stages only. Please be advised that there are no trail signs nor formal routes in existence at this time.

All the material in this section is speculative, except for those public ways or existing trail systems, which already see foot traffic.

The Kingdom of Water

Little Diamond Pond and the string-of-ponds country north of Dixville Notch are a prelude to what stretches ahead on The Cohos Trail. Ponds Gloriette, Abeniki, Mud, Nathan, and Little Diamond, (and Big Diamond over the ridge), are a miniature version of the great bodies of water that lie to the north.

In half a day, the hiker will cross over Ben Young Hill, one of a number of forested ridges which surround the headwater lakes of the Connecticut River. Once over the height of land at Ben Young Hill, the far northern country of New Hampshire is at hand, a land which is kin to the endless lake and low-mountain country of the great majority of the Adirondack National Forest in New York State, outside of the Adirondack's famous "High Peaks" region.

There are dozens of ponds, wetlands, fens, bogs, and lakes in the two townships that make up the Connecticut Lakes Region— Clarksville and Pittsburg. Pittsburg itself is so big—over 300,000 acres—that it is actually the largest town in the continental United States.

Within its borders sprawl four "great" lakes. The southernmost of the giants is Lake Francis, named for a New Hampshire governor. It covers over 2,000 acres. Above it sweeps First Connecticut, a body of water that is 120 feet deep in spots and nearly 3,000-acres big. Climbing in elevation toward the border now, Second Connecticut Lake has dominion. Second Lake, at over 1,200 acres, is the crown jewel of the big four, as there are no structures on its shoreline and the views are of very isolated terrain. And well above Second Lake in vertical elevation sits 800-acre Third Connecticut Lake, a cold, brooding sheet of water under the boundary mountains.

Tucked into the folds of the mountains and ridges of the region are dozens of other water bodies. The biggest is Back Lake, north of Lake Francis and ringed with hotels and camps. There are several large but shallow bog-like features, including beautiful East Inlet northeast of Second Lake, and Moose Flowage, surrounded by spruce and fir spires and bedecked with pink joe-pye weed in mid summer.

There's Round Pond, Mud Pond, Moose Pond, Wright Pond, and on and on. There's Scott Bog and Big Brook Bog, which aren't bogs at all. Then there's Fourth Connecticut Lake, which is really a fen.

A central artery, the Connecticut River, ties the whole of it together. At Fourth Lake, you can actually straddle the river as it leaves the little wetland. By the time the river reaches Lake Francis at Lake Francis Campground, it is a terrific trout stream that is powerful enough to knock you down and sweep you into the lake itself.

Pittsburg has its share of high ground, the highest of which is Stubb Hill. But it's the peak that's just a wee bit lower that gets all the attention. That's 3,360-foot Mt. Magalloway—"the shoveler" (caribou) in Abenaki dialect—seven miles off The Cohos Trail and deep in Dead Diamond country. It sports a good fire tower, a mighty east-facing cliff and talus slope, and marvelous views of the Rangeley Lake country of northeast Maine. It's next door neighbor is 3,000-foot Diamond Ridge, a favorite among snowmobilers. Other peaks linger around 3,000 feet in elevation too, including Rump (mostly in Maine), D'urban, and Salmon on the border, Kent, and Deer, with its abandoned trail to the site of a long-lost fire tower.

Private Property

Most of the lands west and north of Coleman State Park are in the hands of individuals or companies that make their living harvesting timber for the paper pulp industry, or for the saw-log and veneer-log processors in the United States and Canada.

South of the Connecticut Lakes region, land use policies tend to be less strict. But north of Coleman State Park, there are hard and fast rules to play by, and all are advised to heed them.

Most people think that it is only the forest industry itself that restricts use of lands in the north. But actually, the forest industry, the local town governments, the State of New Hampshire, and even the recreation industry players all recognize that the vast forests are the most valuable and critical resource in the far north, not only in terms of raw materials, but in terms of water quality, air quality, wildlife habitat, and quality of human life. All these parties have a big stake in seeing that these forests aren't degraded nor destroyed by human activity, be it development, excessive use of any kind, or fire.

Therefore, the central tenet of land-use policy in Clarksville and Pittsburg is "Day Use Only." All the people and industries of the north welcome traditional uses on the lands during the day, including day-hiking, fishing, hunting, and more recently, snowmobiling and day trail-biking.

But no one on the 45th parallel is going to tolerate camping in the backcountry or fires of any kind at anytime, except during the winter months when snow is on the ground. Camp outside the state campgrounds or private facilities and you will go before a local magistrate at Colebrook, New Hampshire and get the book thrown at you. Light a fire and you risk the same thing. Start a brush or forest fire, and you are going to jail. Plain and simple. But worse, you are going to pay fines and bills from those institutions that had to put out the fire.

Do the Right Thing

Once you leave Coleman State Park for the far north, expect to camp at Lake Francis Campground, Deer Mt. Campground, or any of the private campgrounds and lodges near Lake Francis, First Lake, or Back Lake. In the years ahead, The Cohos Trail Association hopes to erect two or three small lean-tos or other shelters on small parcels of purchased land half way between the string of state park campgrounds. This will make life easier for hikers, but it will also take pressure off landowners who are justifiably nervous about people on large forest tracks after sundown.

The Indian Stream Republic

There is some fascinating history tucked away by the Canadian border, human-made and otherwise. At the head of Pittsburg village is a big earthen dam—Murphy Dam. Below the dam to the west and running away quickly, is the Connecticut River on its 400-mile journey to Long Island Sound. Under the surface waters of the lake that is impounded by Murphy Dam lays a flooded town, where hearty souls once farmed, logged, maintained homes, and sent their children to a two-room school house.

Some of the structures were not removed before the sluice gates at Murphy Dam were closed for good in the '30s.

Most of this little community was moved to make way for the flood-control dam, a Civil Conservation Corp make-work project designed to create lots of jobs and a better life for those living downstream.

But the real story behind the scenes here is that of an independent nation, the Indian Stream Republic. Settlers in Pittsburg once actually lived by their own laws and constitution just after the War of 1812. Then, Canada and the United States were pestering the hardscrabble farmers of the region over a border dispute. A few rebels in town raised a petition to form a sovereign state beholden to neither nation. To their surprise the measure passed on a vote. The Indian Stream Republic was born, complete with its own jail—a huge iron potash kettle turned upside down. Once under it, no soul could lift it by him or herself.

Knowing that history puts a lot of people to sleep, I conclude by saying that the United States didn't care for the region being pestered by Canada, nor did it relish a little puissant republic setting little brushfires in the north woods. So the U.S. and Canada sat down together and agreed to survey the boundary once and for all and cede the land to the Americans. The two governments fixed on Hall's Stream as the western boundary in the region, and the natural mountaintop division of the watersheds of the St. Lawrence River and the Connecticut River as the boundary along the northern U.S. frontier.

To this day, local inhabitants of the Connecticut Lakes region tend to be fiercely independent, anti-government, and doggedly determined to preserve a local culture that is distinctly different from the customs of the down-staters and flatlanders many hours drive to the south. One thing is certain—they don't have much use for body piercing, synco-pop music, or liberal democrats above the 45th parallel.

The Cohos Trail Extension

The Now And Future Cohos Trail

The trail north of Coleman State Park is in the planning stages. It is not complete, but since a great deal of the trail will be confined to public ways, public lands and easements, and some snowmobile trails, the majority of the northern extension of The Cohos Trail can actually be walked now by those who are good at finding their way on unmarked avenues through forest and farmland.

To be sure, there are gaps in the trail plan, and we recommend tramping along isolated stretches of Route 3 or public back roads to work your way north. The guidebook sketches out here the trail plan and its present alternatives so that you know what is possible and what is not.

The Deadwater Bypass

To reach the community of Pittsburg at this time, bypassing the Deadwater region and scooting over Ben Young Hill, a through-hiker must use existing roads and old town lanes to head north. No through trail exists at this time that can be officially called The Cohos Trail.

To move north from Coleman State Park campground, walk south downhill on Diamond Pond Road. Pass a sign for camp E-Toh-Anee and look to the right down off the road. A snowmobile trail known as the Keith Haynes Trail runs in the tamarack and fir here and soon drifts downhill southwest in tight woods, cutting diagonally across state lands, making for the very narrow and tree-shaded Charles Heath Road.

Enter the dirt Charles Heath Road and turn left downhill.

Take that road and walk the long-abandoned farm country road around a low uplift called Paul Hill. Pass a T-intersection near a bar-gate and head left due west as old pasture begins to open up. Cross a small branch of the Mohawk River and pass the Holden Hill Road which cuts off to the right.

Deadwater Country

In the far north, a good number of streams are called dead or deadwater. The name derives from the log driving days. Slow moving water spelled trouble for loggers trying to move logs to market. The thousands of "sticks" in a log drive needed good strong currents to keep them moving and prevent them from binding up into log jams. So the streams and rivers that carry the "dead" moniker were those that were "too damned slow to be of any use to anyone."

Stewartstown's Farm Lanes

The old backcountry farm lanes you are now walking on in the high country of eastern Stewartsown skirt in accordion zig-zag-fashion what is known locally as Deadwater Country. The region north of Mudget Mountain is a frequently logged forest owned by Champion International Corp. Champion has asked the Cohos Trail Association to skirt this low slow drainage basin in favor of higher ground with fine views to the west.

So skip the old lanes north (right) now and stay straight (west) on the narrow Heath Road. It intersects with and becomes the Bear Rock Road just south of a string of narrow shallows called Bear Rock Bog, an alder-filled wetland with a goodly array of wildlife sheltered in the thickets. Turn right onto Bear Rock Road. In a minute, the Noyes Road shuttles in from the left, but stay right and move beyond the bogs, meadowlands, camps, and old farms there. Keep straight and westbound in pasture country as you run just south of a long and broad ridge called Mudget Mountain. The old back lane soon enters the woods and shortly crosses Haines Brook at the junction with Haines Hill Road.

Haines Hill Rd. To Creampoke

At the Haines Hill Road junction, turn right (north) uphill, leaving Bear Rock Road for good. Follow Haines Brook on the right and begin a moderate but steady uphill pace past a cluster of farm buildings and homes. As you climb, the pastures permit

181

views away to the south and east. At the upper pastures, cross the brook, make a tight left turn and head for a gap between North Hill on the west and Mudget Mt. on the east.

Haines Hill Road now narrows down to a one-laner in places and gets rougher. It pushes through forest and abandoned old farmland rising very gradually over an indistinct height of land. It then levels out on a lofty and rather flat landscape that I think of as, and call loosely, the Stewartstown Plateau. There are structures here and there up on the high ground, mostly small, neat camps. Some command wide vistas westward for dozens and dozens of miles and front row seats to stunning sunsets. Begin slowly drifting uphill again and soon the wonderfully named Creampoke Road comes up from the left along a pasture fence. Continue west at over 2,200 feet elevation and take in the stellar views to the left over the slanting pastures southwest, down, down into the Connecticut River valley far below.

To Clarksville Pond

Haines Hill Road stays level along the ridgeline as a few more camps show their faces. Just before the trail slips into the woods for good, take one last look at the grand panorama.

The Route 21 snowmobile corridor rides atop the Haines Hill Road. The road itself ends a mile north of Creampoke Road at a junction with another snowmobile trail coming along on a track once called the East Road. There are various avenues northward from here, but the Cohos Trail Association does not have permission to cross these lands to the vicinity of Clarksville Pond as yet.

So to proceed north, one has to walk west several miles easily downhill on the East Road to rendezvous with Old County Road in high farming country below Kidder Hill. Turn north on Old County Road and amble two miles out to Route 145.

The Abandoned Ferguson Road

If permission is gained, then the trail will cut down a tight dogleg to the east of the East Road trail a short distance in the vicinity of a recent logging operation. Once around the dogleg, the trail branches in a quarter mile. Take the left turn gradually uphill on the Route 21 snowmobile trail. In half a mile, the trail splits again and Route 21 slips away toward the east and the Deadwater Stream while the CT rides what was once known as

Ferguson Road.

This abandoned way now has lots of trees and forest debris down in it, but it is easy to follow over a height of land. Once on the descent, a recent timber cut opens a broad view to the east and northeast to country no one ever sees from this vantage point. Most of the tallest peaks in Pittsburg township can be seen from opposite their traditional vantage points along Route 3 much farther north.

Using my topo maps, I figured I could see Carr Ridge, Mt. Magalloway, Diamond Ridge, Roundtop, and Mt. Pisgah, among others, all from unknown angles.

Ferguson Bog

The old track falls off the ridge and beelines across a crumbling earthen road/dam built over a wetland. The wetland drains through a culvert and around the culvert the roadway is falling apart. A dash across it in a pickup truck would be a mad dash, indeed. At the culvert, look west over Ferguson bog, a nutrient-rich warm water shallow that provides fine habitat for ducks and other waterbirds.

Turn northwestward uphill away from the bog and cross a field with an small abandoned trailer in it, pass another structure in the woods and finally find your way out onto the Clarksville Pond Road.

Clarksville Pond

At the road, turn left (west) on a lane that sits at 2,030 feet elevation. Good pasture opens on the right as the road rises slightly, crowns, and then shuttles past Clarksville Pond, a cold drink of water about half the size of Little Diamond Pond at the base of Ben Young Hill. Several camps and an old campground crowd its eastern shore but they do not seem to bother the ducks that gather on the pond in some numbers.

Should the trail reach Clarksville Pond, plans call for new trail around the west shore where the CT would ramble up a depression between two rounded ridges and venture up and over lofty Ben Young Hill.

Ben Young Hill

Ben Young Hill is too rounded, too sprawling, and too indistinct a summit to be called a mountain. It doesn't reach a pinnacle, or a ledge, or the like. But the views from its heights at the edge of abandoned farms and chance outlooks, make it a must location for the proposed route of the CT.

Today, Ben Young Hill's vistas can be had only from Route 145, as The Cohos Trail Association doesn't have permission to cross the uplands yet. Walking or motoring up Route 145 from the south, one crosses a high ridgeline where the road spikes up steeply and then down steeply all at once. On the crown, views extend north mile after mile into Canada, to the Indian Stream forests in Pittsburg, south toward Colebrook, and well down the Connecticut River valley.

It's the potential for extensive views of rarely seen country that piques one's interest. And Ben Young Hill hides cellar holes and other secrets of a horse-drawn agricultural past that has long since faded away from New England.

It also hides an old, very hard-to-locate logging route which runs northeast just to the north of the height of land and the drive west to the Young radio tower. This old way, on a few 1970 and earlier maps, edges along what are some of New Hampshire's highest elevation farm fields. These clearings open up marvelous vistas to the north and east. Then the route climbs gradually up to a ridgeline between two false summits and begins a descent into a depression that spawns Crawford Brook. It follows Crawford Brook downhill until the way becomes much more distinct and eventually becomes fully developed and houses rise up from the land.

To Pittsburg

To reach Pittsburg now, without trespassing, descend north off the height of land and pace a nondescript two miles on Route 145 until the road bends left suddenly, crosses a small bridge, and enters the little village of Pittsburg. More on Pittsburg in a minute, but whichever way the village is approached, it is essential that you stop here, as it is the first habitation of any kind that one reaches in 100 trail miles of hiking.

The Crawford Road

Plans call for arriving in New Hampshire's northern-most township, and the nation's largest town to boot, via the Crawford Road. This dirt lane backs up southward onto Ben Young Hill from the north about half way to the upland's highest point.

Crawford Road is lined with forest and a few homes on the west side, but its eastern edge runs along great high meadows full of grasses and golden rod in late summer. Over these meadows, 2,000-acre Lake Francis basks in a great depression to the northeast, surrounded by green hills and blue mountains. On the descent, you can see the village of Pittsburg nestled underneath a great earthen dam, which holds back the shimmering lake.

Murphy Dam

Crawford Road empties into the Cedar Stream Road a quarter of a mile west of a slope that anchors the south side of big earthen Murphy Dam. Turn right (east) onto Cedar Stream Road, ascend the ridge, and walk out onto the Civil Conservation Corp dam, built in the '30s as a make-work project to employ local people hit hard by the Depression.

Murphy Dam is a typical earthen, water-control dam with undershot water release, spillway, control tower, and a broad flat, grassy top.

Meander out onto the crest of the quarter-mile long dam and turn your eyes northward across the deep, cold 2,051-acre lake.

Lake Francis

The view across Lake Francis to distant mountains is a primordial vista, even though the lake is less than 70 years old. Everything is shades of blue, green, and white. It looks as if the earth is young, robust, and healthy, the way the continent looked everywhere when there was forest and water before the Europeans opened the land with the steel plow and felling ax.

In my mind, the image is a sort of freeze-frame that "defines" what the North Country is, apart from the White Mountains.

It is hard to believe now that just 35 years ago, some New Hampshire industrialists and politicians tried hard to approve plans for the construction of a nuclear reactor on Lake Francis, to be built after Seabrook Station was finished on the New Hampshire coast or to be built in case Seabrook couldn't be forced down people's throats along the coast.

Pittsburg was chosen for the site for any number of reasons, including plentiful water for cooling, remoteness from human population (and therefore less trouble with on-site protests and evacuation plans), low-level waste disposal potential, and ease of obtaining transmission line right-of-ways from the few large land-owners in the region. We all know now the problems, dangers, high costs, and intractable radioactive material disposal problems associated with nuclear power. But what really killed the project before it got off the ground at Lake Francis was the rumblings of the wise business leaders of the state who were growing angry over paying the highest electric rates in the entire country and even angrier about being told there was no alternative. So much for "cheap" nuclear power.

Looking across the lake, I sometimes envision this world on a 40-below zero morning with two nuclear power cooling towers dwarfing Mt. Magalloway in the distance. From the tops of the towers, great columns of white steam rise straight up a mile into the still, painfully cold air. The high-tension wires hum. And Lake Francis lies black and steaming, its waters not quite cold enough

Lake Francis in Pittsburg, NH.

to freeze solid (as they surely always do now) because the cooling towers don't quite get the job done before their above-freezing waters are piped into the lake.

Pittsburg Village

Walk across Murphy Dam to the north and swing left on a tight loop that brings you down to the base of the dam. Walk out the access road, climb a little rise, and slip out onto Route 3 not far from the recently renovated Pittsburg Public School. Turn left (south) on Route 3 and enter the little village immediately, with its several restaurants, post office, general store, and a smattering of town buildings. In Pittsburg you may buy supplies for the continuing trek, or purchase a hot meal and a beer.

Or turn right (north) on Route 3 and walk a mile or so to the first private campground along the road. There you may tent and pick up a few things, as well.

Pittsburg has the feel of a frontier town. It's not a classic New England charmer with white steepled churches and aging stone walls. Rather, it fits like an old worn pair of shoes that you like and won't part with.

Cedar Stream Road

Once resupplied in Pittsburg Village, retrace your steps back to Murphy Dam. Cross the wide top of the dam to the south this time, and turn left (east) onto Cedar Stream Road.

Cedar Stream Road was built as a logging tote road many decades ago and it is still used a great deal for that purpose. Logging trucks are common when harvests are underway in the nearby woods, and the trucks have the right of way at all times. Walk a mile on this dirt avenue in woods the whole way, until the road dips sharply downhill to cross a stout bridge over Labrador Brook. From the bridge, you are quite a height off the water and you get a good look at a wild mountain stream, which drains one of the more dismal swamplands in all of the north. After the first mile, the road swings in close to the lake and pleasant views poke out to the north across the waters. Pass camps on your left and a few on your right as the trees begin to close in over the road, providing nice shade most of the way. Cedar Stream Road begins to take on the persona of a lazy, pleasant country lane and holds it for most of the remaining miles.

Eventually, the lake begins to broaden out rapidly as a long northern inlet opens out across the land to where Lake Francis Campground resides unseen at the far end. In half a mile, the lake narrows again as the eastern shore begins to catch up with you. Soon you are walking through woods on both sides, the lake now behind you. At mile six from the dam, the road swings easily to the right while a spur road hangs left down a slight depression. Turn left off Cedar Brook Road onto the old route, which has now grown entirely to grasses.

Bog Branch Trail (Dead End)

The old track is the Bog Branch tote road. It tracks straight a minute to a turnabout. On the left is a gate. Cross through the gate and cross a plank bridge over one of two branch streams entering Lake Francis in this area. Pass a camp with a humorous sign or two on the left and come to a second bridge.

The bridge is the end of the line, for now. You may walk on grassy state easements for approximately another 4,000 feet, crossing a few snowmobile bog bridges over wet areas, but new trail must be constructed down toward the lake shore and north to where the Connecticut River enters Lake Francis.

The Cohos Trail Association envisions some sort of bridge across the Connecticut River just upstream from the campground, probably a good-size suspension bridge. But building such a structure is a tall order, both in terms of dollars and commitments from the association, U.S. Generating of New England, and state agencies, as well.

Don't look for a structure any time soon, and don't cross the river here in moderate to high water. Excellent trout-fishing can be found here, but the river can be very powerful and knock your feet out from underneath you.

Lake Francis State Campground

It is easy to reach Lake Francis Campground from Route 3, traveling south on the River Road for a mile right down into the facility on the lake. It is home to the obligatory creosote brown headquarters building, land yacht (camper) spots, and tent platforms out in the woods. A new all-purpose building was built in 1999.

Check in at the office to purchase a tent platform rental for the evening. Then walk northeast to where the campground narrows and a trail enters the woods and finds its way out to the river. Platforms are placed here and there. They escaped damage recently when a severe windstorm took down some of the larger trees standing around each of the platforms.

Trek upstream for a few hundred feet and enjoy the rushing Connecticut River, here a hard driving waterway that is dangerous to cross. It is in this vicinity that The Cohos Trail Association hopes that someday a bridge, which accommodates one person at a time, can be built in a graceful suspended arch above the froth.

River Road Trail

To leave the campground for the north, you may follow the River Road up to Route 3 or walk a little snowmobile trail that hugs fairly tight to the road right of way. The route keeps you off the road, at least. Soon pass directly over the Carr Ridge Road, a major forest tote lane, and swing close to the old River Road covered bridge, the northern-most such span in New Hampshire.

Young's Store

The trail begins to rise after the bridge and within half a mile swings alongside Route 3 near the site of a venerable North Country institution, Young's Store.

Perched on a bluff overlooking First Connecticut Lake, a good half mile south of the River Road junction, Young's is one of those you-can-get-anything-you-want stores that invariably open for business in the far places, where populations are thin and road miles long to the nearest town. Such a place is Young's Store.

I always stop in. I buy this and that, but sometimes I just roam quietly in the store and watch the marvelous array of Homo sapiens that cascade in and out of the place in every season. In winter it's snowmobile heaven here despite the hellish noise from the Formula 1 sleds. Springtime is fishing season and you can't fish here without a license from Young's. Tourists, not quite by the droves, stop by after "moosin'" up the line. And in the fall an orange army rolls in with big rifles arrayed in orderly fashion in the rear window of every pickup truck.

Young's is a gold mine. It has to be. It's not pretty, but the dollars must run deep like the lakes, and I don't have any problem adding a few greenbacks to the depths.

First Lake Spillway

After your blissful experience at Young's Store, toddle alongside Route 3 northeast this time a long mile, pass a cemetery, and watch several bright white clapboard houses reveal themselves on the left and a dark, massive concrete and steel monolith rear up on the right. You can hear this dam before you see it. It's the impoundment that holds back vast First Connecticut Lake.

Enter a small parking area at the head of the dam. There are log railings ahead. Walk up to them and peer down. Leaping from the middle of the great dam is a torrid flume, which crashes to the rocks below and fills a little canyon with spray and a fine whitewash mist. The land hums with low frequency vibrations pounded out by the falling water. Low water levels dampened down the experience the last time I saw the spillway, but still the sight and rumble was impressive. In high water, the spillway is a powerful magnet, drawing you in to be coated with mist and drenched in sound and liquid fury.

First Connecticut Lake Dam is an old timer, its surface concrete crumbling, and inviting footing for lichen and mosses. The structure was built not to create the huge lake but to increase its size to power log drives.

U.S. Gen Picnic Grounds

Just beyond the dam U.S. Generating of New England maintains a broad picnic area at the edge of the lake. Ducks and seagulls have learned that humans can't resist feeding wildlife, so there is always a bevy of our avian friends at the picnic area.

Walk down to the lake just to the right of a little round peninsula knob that supports a few evergreens. Take a look out across the lake to the northeast to Hedgehog Nubble, the north flanks of Diamond Ridge and Stub Hill, and distant Mt. Prospect, all standing about with blue coats on.

But better views await you a little farther north. Get your feet out of the cold lake water, work into your hiking boots and walk off on the footway that squeezes between the lake and the road for half a mile on U.S. Gen. easements. As you climb out away from the lake and crest a ridge, a panoramic view sweeps away 180-degrees to all points east.

First Connecticut Lake

Route 3 banks into a big bend to the left to get around a large rounded inlet that backs up against the hill to Ramblewood Campground and Cabins and Magalloway Cabins. On the banks of this slackwater, one of the storied vistas of the far north expands to the east. Photographers love this spot, because the view frames near and distant shores and the massive, but graceful, mountain king, Magalloway.

Everything looks big here. For the first time you really get a sense of just how big this largest of the Connecticut Lakes is. How they measure these things I'll never know, but First Lake is 2,807 acres big, and at several soundings is a cold and dark 120-feet deep. It is the second largest lake in New Hampshire north of Lake Winnepesauke. Only Umbagog, well to the southeast, is larger. But First Lake holds more water, because Umbagog is little more than a puddle in depth over most of its great girth.

First Lake has the very thing that Umbagog does not, a great mountain peak looming over its waters, which gives the whole valley a sense of grandeur and drama. Umbagog is so shallow that it supports lots of warm water species, while First Lake is frightfully cold almost all year and is home to cold-loving rainbow and lake trout and the locally much-prized land-locked salmon.

Magalloway Cabins

When looking across First Lake, directly behind you is Route 3 and a slope which rises continuously northward to a low summit called Covill Mountain. At the foot of this slope, just above Route 3, is Magalloway Cabin, reached by the Young Road and Ramblewood Road. The resort welcomes CT hikers as well as trail bikers, cross-country skiers, and snowmobilers in winter.

Magalloway Cabins has agreed to act has a hiker hostel on the Cohos Trail system. To get their special rate, just tell them you are hiking the CT and would like a special reservation for a CT trekker.

The Brundage Forest

Once across Route 3, enter Young Road and in a minute turn right onto Ramblewood Road, which forks to the left in a few more feet. This old road is the access to the Brundage Forest and

French Wildlife Reserve. The Brundage acreage, most of the south flank of Covill Mt., is in the hands of the Society for the Protection of New Hampshire Forests (SPNHF), a venerable conservation organization operating for nearly 100 years which manages many thousands of acres of critical habitat in the state.

Brundage Forest cradles a small body of water known either as Mud Pond or Eagle Pond, depending on which map you peruse. There are so many Mud Ponds in the state, that I vote for the little sheet of water being named Eagle Pond.

The lane rises to a good size south-facing clearing, which looks down on all 2,807 acres of First Connecticut Lake.

Round Pond

At this point, the trail is incomplete. There is an old tote road that runs under the crest of the mountain and east toward Round Pond, a full glacier-scoop on the order of the size of Little Diamond Pond. Round Pond is tucked into a horseshoe ring of low-forested ridges and drained by a good stream that goes by the same name. The track arrives at the wooded western shore, which lies just outside the SPNHF's Brundage lands.

The Cohos Trail Association does not yet have permission to follow the tote road east and a similar old passage on the way out to Route 3 at the very southern tip of the boundary of New Hampshire's long and narrow Connecticut Lakes State Forest. If the association can work out a trail on these existing ways here, it opens the way to rarely visited terrain, panoramic views, and a fine mountain tarn and good wildlife habitat.

Connecticut Lakes State Forest

Standing at the edge of Route 3, there are lots of options for new trails, but only one way to go—at least for now. Route 3 runs north for 20 miles to the border inside a 1,000-foot-wide easement that is bordered by Champion International Corp. forests on all sides and in some cases by equally narrow easements managed by U.S. Generation. Both the state and the power company had similar things in mind when they worked out the easements in the far north. The state wanted to create a forest buffer between the road and the timber country to preserve a sense of unfettered wilderness, while the utility was charged with protecting the riparian corridors around the lakes and along the Connecticut River and Smith Brook.

These easements succeed well in creating the illusion that there is an unbroken wilderness outside the Sunday drive windshield. That illusion is strengthened greatly by the fact that moose, early every morning and every evening come out of these easements to graze along the road and river. In the spring, moose frequent the roadsides to find road salt washed into the highway margins. They crave sodium and they find it in abundance. These great animals reinforce the notion that there is a wild continent stretching away to the North Pole.

Big Timber Country

But the Pittsburg forests are so-called working forests, meaning they are harvested periodically, usually in 30- to 40- year cycles. Most of the cuts are under 100 acres and create a patchwork quilt of different age stands of trees that most wildlife, particularly the larger mammals, find very much to their liking. The cuttings open the forest floor to light, allowing low-browse berries and grasses to come in for a period of time before the trees overtop and shade out the low growth. The surge of light after a cut fuels a profusion of growth that moose, deer, bear, and other mammals thrive on. Consequently the numbers of many of these creatures have increased significantly in the last half-century.

The paper and saw log industry has been, until recently, very shy about opening land to hikers and trail-bikers. These companies have been blamed for a host of ills in the past, but there is a growing sense in the conservation community and in the recreation community that the large forestland owners, at least in the northeast, have contributed mightily to keeping vast tracts of land open and in trees. Consequently, an extensive wooded environment stretches from the Gaspe Peninsula of Quebec, across most of Maine, half of New Hampshire and Vermont, much of eastern New York State, a good deal of Pennsylvania, and all the way down the back of the Blue Ridge Mountains of Virginia to the Great Smokies.

This 2,000 mile contiguous forest rims the greatest concentration of people in the continental United States. Conservationists see this eastern forest as the first true grand-scale reforestation success in the worldwide forests conservation effort. If a high-tech society of 100 million people can live in very close proximity to hundreds of thousands of square miles of undeveloped forest land, then perhaps there is hope for forests everywhere.

Logging and Conservation

Logging cuts aren't pretty, of course. But the relatively small cuts typical in northern New Hampshire generally do not have the aesthetic impact nor the impact on wildlife habitat that occurs in places like the Olympic peninsula of Washington State, where mile after mile of forest is clear cut and timber companies and environmental groups clash regularly and heatedly over a harvesting practice that everyone outside the industry loathes.

In suburban Atlanta and Charlotte, many hundreds of square miles of forest are being leveled each decade as these exploding cities chew into the environment. Such boom towns across America are creating whole new communities where the needs of automobiles—roads, parking, service centers, and their attendant retail onslaught—devour land out of all proportion to the populations, which move onto those newly accessible acres.

The forests on these lands are divided and divided into smaller and smaller parcels until the forest simply can't sustain any creatures except small rodents and insects. Habitats collapse over enormous areas. Contrast this to what you see on The Cohos Trail in sustained-yield logging tracts in northern Coos County. Moose are everywhere and flourishing, as are deer and black bear. Rivers and lakes are clean and clear. Rare species, like the pine marten, in protected boreal forests above 2,700 feet, are recovering.

In the East, and particularly in northern New Hampshire, something else is going on. The creation of the Nash Stream Forest at the heart of The Cohos Trail was a catalyst for a large-scale land conservation movement that is seeing large tracts of land set aside under conservation easements and holdings. A number of timber companies operating in New Hampshire have, in the last two decades, divested themselves of isolated parcels of their lands—sometimes blocks of many thousands of acres. In recent years, most of these parcels have been purchased outright by conservation associations. Individuals too, with large holdings are often willing to donate large blocks of land to conservation causes.

In the '90s alone, thousands of acres have been added to the White Mountains National Forest and thousands more bordering the forest have been protected. Surrounding the Nash Stream Forest, many thousands of acres of former Champion International lands have come under conservation easements, and these lands will be managed wisely so that the properties are productive in terms of timber and wildlife habitat protection, recreational use, and water quality.

It has become well recognized on all sides—in industry, government, in recreation, and conservation circles—that multiple uses can be maintained within a forest environment and that all parties, including the wild creatures that live there, can benefit. Mead Corporation, in particular, has embraced this new forest ethic and maintains it as a matter of management policy throughout northern New Hampshire. Champion International has voluntarily set aside thousands of acres of their lands in Pittsburg, providing for protection of such critical or unique environments as the woodlands around Fourth Connecticut Lake, East Inlet, and Norton Preserve, and the Connecticut Lakes State Forest. International Paper has a novel lease agreement with Mountain Recreation Corporation, which permits a recreation industry to coexist with the firm within the forested tracts in the Phillips Brook valley.

Things are changing fast. Every few months there's a headline about a new transaction that sets land aside for good, freeing it forever from the threat of development. The people of northern New Hampshire will be the beneficiaries (and so will the rest of the state and visitors to the region, of course) of these recent policies and practices that will ensure that these great tracts of land continue to exist as productive multiple-use woodlands.

The Dead Diamond Country

Once The Cohos Trail leaves the Covill Mt. area, the trail runs north toward the border. But there are a few traditional destinations this far north that hikers might want to see that are many miles off the CT. On the northeastern end of First Connecticut Lake, Champion International Corp. maintains a no-nonsense logging thruway known as the Magalloway Road. It is the best way in to a vast isolated territory drained southeastward by numerous branch streams of the Dead Diamond River system. High, long ridges and mountains abound, including Mt. Magalloway with its fine summit and fire tower some seven miles down the Magalloway Road. And well beyond Magalloway the timber company maintains a little trail to a rarely seen, but impressive cascade known as Garfield Falls.

Mt. Magalloway

Follow signs for seven miles on the Magalloway Road southeast to the base of big Mt. Magalloway, named for the Abenaki Indian word for "woodland caribou," which are extinct in New England. A sign guides you from the lane to a jeep trail directly up the mountain. The going is easy and the ascent is surprisingly quick.

The trail rounds out and enters a large grassy clearing just east of the summit of the mountain. The clearing is flat and pleasant and supports a working fire tower and the watchman's cabin (still in good repair). In 1978, the watchman at the time, a fellow named LaMontagne (if I remember correctly) from the tiny New Hampshire city of Berlin (BURR-lun), cooked up a calorie-laden, four-course lunch. It was a fantastic treat on a beautiful North Country day. The conversation is forgotten but it was the sort of conversation one has that, while its underway, gives one the feeling that everything is perfectly right with the world.

Continue east on level ground to the eastern cliff ledges that Magalloway is famous for. Much of the east side of the peak is vertical, hard granite wall and vast rubble-strewn talus slope. The view is excellent, with the 17-mile ribbon of Aziscoos Lake and the other big lakes in the Rangley system visible well to the east.

Everywhere are forested peaks, the most prominent being Rump Mountain, about 200 feet taller than Magalloway just over the Maine line to the northeast. Rump Mountain is a bushwhacker's dream, so remote is it. Bosebuck, Deer Mt., and Mt. Aziscoos (all in Maine), frame the Maine lakes. On the best days, near the eastern horizon, you can make out Maine's 4,000-footers, Sugarloaf, Crocker, Saddleback, and the Bigelow Range.

Magalloway Tower

Climb the well-maintained fire tower to the tower cabin (if it's open) or to the highest stairwell and take in a majestic view of the other points of the compass. Below, to the northwest and to the southwest, the big string of lakes you've been skirting—the Connecticut Lakes—sun themselves amidst a panoply of forest and peak. Almost no structures or farm clearings are visible, only an occasional woods road or camp along a lake. Here and there sizable harvest cuts show as odd shaped parcels in the landscape.

Due west on the western horizon is Vermont's Jay Peak. New Hampshire's own Deer Mt. (one of many with the same name), stands over Third Connecticut Lake to the northeast. Beyond the boundary mountains to the north, you can see a flat horizon—the St. Lawrence River Valley in Quebec. To the south the landscape is a wrinkled carpet of the peaks and valleys you have been working your way over for days. You can just make out the Northeast Peaks, and the Pilot and Pliny Ranges in the haze on the extreme horizon. They hide the higher Presidential Range from view.

The reason why Mt. Magalloway is one of the great spots becomes apparent if you motor in from nearby Lake Francis Campground and hike up for a fine sunrise on a late summer morning. Air inversions are common in late summer in the north, and clouds hug the land in the valleys and around the lakes. The air is usually clear of clouds above, and chilly.

The ground-cloud effect is magnified when it's very early and the sun (below the horizon) has set the low horizon aglow with hot reds. Then the forests around Magalloway are a deep electric blue. The valleys are shimmering, silver pools of land clouds, and the edge of the world frames it all in colors of hot, wood-stove coals.

Pretty heady stuff.

Garfield Falls

In the days of the river drives, Garfield Falls was one of those places feared by the river drivers. The falls themselves were dangerous in the spring runoff, but more troublesome was the tendency for floating logs to jam tightly at the top or bottom of the falls. These jams had to be "picked" apart by men using pike poles, or when all else failed, by use of dynamite.

Freeing a jam was treacherous work. Sometimes the log dam would breakup suddenly, catching a workman by surprise. If he fell, it was sure, sudden death. Garfield Falls was one of several such squeeze-hole falls through which drivers had to work their logs. Another, not too far away, earned the name Hellgate. Both falls killed their share of men. Today Garfield Falls is managed for its rugged beauty and a tiny, rain forest-like community of water-loving plants that enjoy a constant bath of spray rising from the falls.

Where Do We Go From Here

After leaving the Covill Mountain area and before the Magalloway Road enters Route 3 on the right, The Cohos Trail has four avenues open to it, only one of which—Route 3 itself—can now be used as a right of way north.

New trail will likely be built at the end of a dirt drive down to old Camp Otter resort on First Connecticut Lake. This new path would follow the north shore of First Lake in U.S. Generating (now PG&E, as the company was just sold) easements to the inlet of the Connecticut River. There are handsome views of unspoiled shoreline at every turn. Once at the river, the trail would cross over nearby Magalloway Road and move upstream. The power company has agreed to permit a new trail in forests near the north bank of the river up to Second Connecticut Lake. If the trail is constructed, it will probably be ready by summer of 2001.

Until this new trail is complete, the way north is now along Route 3 over ten miles to Deer Mountain Campground north of Second Connecticut Lake. Do not fret too much, as the road is very scenic, very little traveled, and is a haunt for moose.

The last two options are centered around the narrow 20-mile Connecticut Lakes State Forest. Either a new trail would be cut in the 1,000-foot wide right of way, or the trail itself would simply follow alongside the road. Whatever option comes to pass, it will likely be at least one and probably two years before a woods trail can be completed here.

Second Connecticut Lake

Five miles beyond the Route 3-Magalloway Road junction, a small version of the First Lake dam comes into view on the right. It possesses a miniature spillway but nowhere near the drama of First Lake's outlet. The dam was built, like the one 15 miles south, to increase the size of a natural lake, the bulk of which lays hidden in the trees to the northeast.

A short distance after the dam, a spur road cuts right for Second Connecticut Lake's boat-access landing. Walk a quarter mile and take a right downhill to a small parking area, turn left and take a look at the jewel of the Connecticut Lakes region.

Second Lake is the charmer of the chain of lakes that makes up the headwaters of the Connecticut River. There are only a handful of camps at Idlewilde, only a couple near the shoreline. There are three islands and two prominent peninsulas. The lake is 61 feet deep at its deepest depth and the surface of the lake is 1,871 feet above sea level. A boat ramp built for small, low-horsepowered motor craft or canoes is here. This is a lake for serious anglers, and expert anglers like a quiet, undisturbed environment.

Of the four big lakes in the chain, Second Lake feels like it's the most remote. Third Lake to the north is so much smaller that it lacks the drama of Second Lake. Lake Francis and First Lake are bustling with human activity in camps along their northern shores. Second Lake is big and it's quiet. The developed country to the south has been left behind. During the weekdays, you will see no one on the lake almost any time of year. On the weekends you'll get a few boats, and often they will be at the mouth of the streams, off the broad open expanse of water, where the fishing is best.

East Inlet and Norton Reserve

Work your way from the lake out to Route 3 again. Turn right and pad along a mile to a dirt road running to the right. Keep left on the CT and head for Deer Mountain Campground. Or, if you are adventurous, take the right turn and ramble 1.2 miles to little East Inlet flowage dam, which affords a pleasant view across narrow shallows to 3,647-foot Rump Mountain.

The road to the right of the dam has been opened for snowmobilers and pedal-trail bikers, but not for long-distance hikers. A hiker attempting to visit Boundary Pond or Rump Mountain simply can't get in and get out in one day. If you wish to visit these very remote areas, bring a trail bike to Deer Mountain Campground.

But East Inlet holds a wonderful secret for hikers, snowshoers and cross-country skiers: Norton Reserve. Step back a few hundred feet from the dam and pick up the trail around the north side of East Inlet. The trail works northeast around the wetland pond and enters a very special parcel of forest indeed. Norton Reserve is a 400+ acre-block of wild wetland and forest. It has been set aside because in some parts of the area there are a few

199

remaining remnants of the original primordial forest that once covered all of eastern North America. It is a gift for outdoor lovers and for scientists alike.

Here you can enter another world altogether. The great softwood trees are fairly numerous and some are enormous, some towering well over 100 feet tall. Few easterners have ever seen such a forest.

Two things become immediately apparent. There are two forests here. One is a fern and fungus understory of pale greens that carpet the forest floor, growing in the dim, moist light that filters down. The second forest is far above you, way up there 50 feet out of reach. Only giant shafts of gray tree trunks connect the two.

Such a battalion of big, white pines were once the favored trees of English and American navies. The giants were originally set aside and then felled for main masts on sailing ships. Throughout the region, most of the large white pines have long since been cut for timber. While once they were so common that Coos County was named for the Abenaki word for pine tree, the white pines now take a back seat to spruce and fir on the heights and in the deep valleys, and to hardwoods on the slopes.

Norton Reserve is a mystical place, almost unearthly. It has a "soft" quiet to it, although tiny drops of sap and upper story detritus rain down constantly on warm summer days. The air is rich in moisture and earthy odors, and it's cool all the time. The place feels "right" like no place I've ever been, except perhaps the Olympic Rain Forest east of Seattle.

Deer Mountain Campground

Get back to Route 3 and cross the road to the west. A short snowmobile trail link runs uphill and to the north. Walk this link under a knob called Black Cat Spur, and eventually descend to a bar-gate just off Route 3. This gate bars vehicles from entering Moose Flowage country, but it is open in the winter for skimobiles running the state-long Route 5 snowmobile trail.

Walk up Route 3 a few hundred feet to the sign for Deer Mountain Campground, a quaint, small facility maintained by the state in this most-isolated of regions. Walk in the driveway to the left and come to the tiny red-shingled camp headwaters with its

Walk up Route 3 a few hundred feet to the sign for Deer Mountain Campground, a quaint, small facility maintained by the state in this most-isolated of regions. Walk in the driveway to the left and come to the tiny red-shingled camp headwaters with its wiry radio antenna tower.

If you reach Deer Mountain Campground, you must overnight here. There are no facilities anywhere else and camping in the woods in the region is strictly forbidden. Set up a tent on the ground along the wetlands of Moose Flowage behind the campground. There are no tent platforms.

Moose Flowage

Deer Mountain Campground rests at the tail of a narrow marshy, wetlands environment. The atmosphere in summer is usually full of moisture and dew collects on everything. In the morning, shake yourself or your tent off and collect yourself for the last leg of your journey.

As has been the case since your day at Coleman State Park, there is no formal Cohos Trail in the far north. It is still in the planning stages.

Deer Mountain Campground office.

swings west and north around the extensive wetlands in the area. The CT hopes to be able to use this several mile link to the border or cut a new trail near Route 3 that dodges down to the wetlands occasionally for a look 'round.

The old road, which doubles as a major snowmobile trail, is largely level and an easy, pleasant walk. In the summer, pink joe-pye weed blossoms line the way, contrasting with the black green spruce and fir. As you walk north, views of backwater marshes occur regularly framed by the boundary mountains behind. The wetland is a collecting basin, which culminates at Third Connecticut Lake two miles ahead. Here the waters that give rise to the Connecticut River organize for the big push 400 miles to the sea.

Deer Mountain (3,005 Feet)

On your left as you go, 3,005-foot Deer Mountain looms, one of the taller peaks in the far north. Skimobile trail now runs up its eastern flank and crosses a height of land a quarter mile from the summit and then disappears down into Perry Stream valley.

Some of this snow-machine trail was once part of a service road that led to a fire tower on the summit of Deer Mt. The tower has long since been abandoned and taken down, so the way to the actual summit is closed and hard to find, let alone follow. Where once you could get a wonderful view from the fire tower of New Hampshire's most isolated regions, there are only restricted views from openings along the snowmobile track.

Some souls still make a destination of Deer Mt. But a trek must be a day trip. You cannot camp on the private lands here. Please do not fail to heed this notice, as you will jeopardize the entire Cohos Trail system in the far north if you do.

Walk by Deer Mt. and head north in the valley on the west side of Moose Flowage and work your way easily uphill toward Third Connecticut Lake in prime moose country. The trail swings left as you approach this 800-acre basin, runs west around a small bay, then jogs north again along the western shore. Work your way down to the water in several places for a look at this big, brooding pond, the last of the "great" lakes in the Connecticut Lakes region. Across the waters is a ridge overtopped by a summit several miles away called Salmon Mt. The U.S.-Canadian boundary runs over the very top of this wooded crest. On the west side of Third Lake, cross an inconspicuous stream on your way north to Route 3. This is the Connecticut River, what little of it there is.

The trail increases in elevation as the lake retreats. It climbs a ridge and meets Route 3 about 2,000 feet below a pronounced height of land. Walk north on the west side of Route 3 with a rock ledge outcropping uphead on the border. The road eases left and crowns the height of land at a little brick-and-wood U.S. Customs Station with its car portal. If you are coming out of Canada by car you must stop here.

Hikers should report too, sign a little guest book, and tell the agent where you are headed.

Fourth Connecticut Lake

The final destination in the far north is actually a two-acre fen, a bog-like area with clear flowing water, which sits in a mountain bowl under a steep boundary ridge. From the Customs Station, walk north a few feet in the direction of the Canadian Station 1,000 feet north, then turn left at the little sign signaling the trailhead for the Fourth Lake Trail.

The trail actually works its way steadily uphill along the border itself. The demarcation between the two countries is a 60-foot swath cut in the forests. At the center of the swath you will see little bronze markers which signify the "line in the sand."

Follow this swath half a mile, when the trail pitches off the ridge to the left and descends steeply and quickly down to a hollow where little Fourth Lake resides. The way down gives silent testimony to the power and destructive force of the 1998 ice storm. Trees everywhere here were crippled, shattered, and toppled. It took a considerable effort to reopen the little trail in to Fourth Lake.

In the hollow you are greeted by a modest little sheet of water, which is hemmed in by spruce and fir, grasses, shrubs, and wild flowers. This is the starting gate for the Connecticut River. The Nature Conservancy protects the land and the pond, a gift from Champion International Corp.

Fourth Lake is also the finish line for The Cohos Trail. If and when the formal trail is opened from Coleman State Park to the border, this little wet spot, tucked so far away from the hustle and bustle, is the culmination point of the 160-mile journey.

The Boundary Mountains

The country on the border is little explored. To walk the boundary for some miles, you must first check in with U.S. Customs and tell them your intention. Since there is some occasional smuggling in remote corners along the border, do not be surprised if there is some consternation about your activity.

East of the U.S. Customs Station there are a number of named and unnamed summits that divide the waters between Canada and the United States. The boundary clearing runs on the divide and eventually finds its way to a boundary monument at the three-way Maine, New Hampshire, and Quebec borders.

Because the boundary way is wide, amounting to a cleared summit for mile after mile, good views are possible in many directions, and you can reach some interesting ledges and very remote Boundary Pond, where customs officials are forced to monitor activity because it is a known smuggling point.

The French Connection

An Eccentric Character

At the Mountain View House at Whitefield, New Hampshire, I had the good fortune to chat with several of the Canadian Premiers (governors) of the provinces of eastern Canada. One of the gentlemen had his dress jacket off, his sleeves rolled up and his tie askew. His gray hair lay matted to one side over his forehead, the strands filled with smoke from an endless chain of cigarettes he kept going.

His name was Rene Levesque, Quebec's Premier and the father of the Quebecquois, the French Canadian separatist party.

This little fellow burned so brightly in a room with his countrymen and with governors from the six New England states, that the others had to blink often. He was fiercely nationalistic, and wanted French Canada to have a sovereign state of its own, and that state would be Quebec and its capital would be Quebec City.

Several hours south of Quebec City, a town that is altogether European in culture and cuisine, the broad plains of the St. Lawrence River run up against a winding wall of 3,000-foot peaks along the New Hampshire and Maine border. From the Quebec side they are more impressive than from the U.S. side, because there are no other mountains in the way and you are standing much closer to sea level.

As the crow flies north of the boundary some 40 miles, a massive circular upthrust formation rams up out of the flat farmlands. On a topographical map of the region, the thing is astonishing because it is as perfectly round a mountain formation as nature could hew out of the earth. It is Mont Megantic, one of the largest peaks in L'Estrie, the eastern townships of Quebec.

Mont Megantic is much loved by a group of French Canadian hikers who formed a trail development organization called Sentiers Frontaliers (Trails of the Frontier or Wild Trails). From its slopes they have been constructing paths in southerly directions to Mont

Third Connecticut Lake and Deer Mountain, Pittsburg, NH.

205

Marble on the Maine border, and toward Mt. D'Urban, a 3,000-footer on the New Hampshire line.

The Sentiers Frontaliers have been in periodic communication with the Cohos Trail Association. Both groups would like to someday link their trail systems together to form one of the first international trails in the east.

Invading Quebec

Should the trail groups actually succeed in developing a conjoined system, such a system might look something like this to the hiker.

At the border, after checking in with the U.S. Customs officials, you would have to cross over the border and proceed 600 feet to the Canadian customs office at the crest of Magnetic Hill. There you would have to sign in as well, because you will be entering the country and you can't enter legally unless you go through the allotted checkpoint. Once the pleasantries are through, walk east to the boundary clearing and rise on the elevated divide between the two nations.

There are two major peaks on the way, Mt. Salmon and Mt. D'Urban, both which afford wide views from the boundary clearing. Near Mt. D'Urban, the Canadians want to push through a trail that falls down D'Urban's north flank and runs in woods and soon in farmland in a northerly direction. The trail zigzags on old farm lanes a while before skirting along the wooded Riviere Au Saumon river down to the Riviere Chesham branch.

There the trail crosses the river and follows the branch stream in forest to the foot of Mont Megantic. The destination is not the summit, although there is no reason not to climb to the top of the fine peak.

The real prize is a great white dome-shaped building, l'observatorie astronomique, a classic astronomical observatory on the east flank of the mountain.

Once at the home of the telescope, you have traveled more than 200 miles, if you've started your trek at the Davis Path trailhead five miles south of Crawford Notch. The door to the stars is the final footfall.

The Trail's End...

If you are like most mortals, you have a blister or two and you are tired of days of non-stop gorp consumption (because the good grub ran out a while ago). If the weather has been pleasant, you are probably elated and want to celebrate. If the weather has been foul—it certainly can be—you are probably cold, physically drained, slightly depressed, and a bit, well, snippy.

Hopefully, the trip will have changed your perspective on how humans should live their lives in the environment. You may decide that such places really are essential to keep at bay the ravages of a consumer culture that values fast food joints over the forest fastness.

We need huge blocks of undeveloped—not necessarily unproductive—lands that provide unbroken habitat for wildlife and wild plants, that provide natural filters for cleaning water and air, that sustain timber and fiber resources, and that provide low-impact recreational opportunities. We need space. Big space. And where it's essential, we even need wild spaces that are left altogether alone.

The Cohos Trail rummages around in the soul of New Hampshire's big spaces. The path shows you the very beautiful face of a healthy, natural environment that is not completely without the wrinkles and scars left by humans. The trail itself has negligible impact upon the land, but I suspect the land you see along the way will seep into your recesses and take over your senses and soul completely.

What could be better?

CXCXCX

LISTS

Cohos Trail Reference Information

Reference Lists

In this section, you can see at a glance, lists of physical features along The Cohos Trail, arranged from the south northward. If you were to hike the CT the entire distance, you could expect these features to show up as you tick off the miles. Also listed are human-made features and lists of supplies you'll need for a through hike on the CT.

Natural Features

Waterfalls And Spillways

1. Dry River Falls, Montalban Range, Dry River Valley
2. Upper Falls, Ammonoosuc River, Base Station Rd.
3. Lower Falls, off Rte. 302 south of Cherry Mt. Rd.
4. Devil's Hopyard, tiny cascade at far wall of gorge
5. Pond Brook Falls, Nash Stream Road, on Pond Brook
6. Huntington Falls, two falls in gorge at Dixville Notch
7. Flume Cascade, rugged little flume at Dixville Notch
8. First Connecticut Lake Dam, powerful water release, Pittsburg
9. Second Connecticut Lake Dam, miniature version of First Lake dam, Pittsburg
10. Moose Falls, small cascade below Route 3, Pittsburg

Terminus Points/Trailheads

1. Davis Path Trailhead South of Crawford Notch. Parking
2. Mt. Washington Hotel Bretton Woods. Park with permission
3. Bretton Woods Depot Fabyans Depot. Parking
4. Upper Falls pull out Crawford Purchase. East of falls 1/8 mi.
5. Zealand campground. Twin Mt. Park across from sites
6. Owlshead Trailhead, Jefferson. Route 115, Parking
7. Starr King Trailhead, Jefferson. Off Route 2. Parking
8. South Pond Rec. Area, Stark. Off Route 110. Parking
9. Bald Mt. Trailhead. Pull off Percy Rd., 100' east of bar-gate
10. Christine Lake, Christine Lake Rd., off Percy Road
11. Percy Peaks Trailhead, Nash Stream Forest. Parking
12. Percy Loop Trailhead. Park but don't block drive to camp
13. Pond Brook Falls. Pullout on Nash Stream Road
14. Sugarloaf Trailhead, Stratford. Park just off road
15. Nash Stream Headwaters Rd. Odell. Park away from gate
16. Dixville Notch trailheads, Dixville Notch. Parking
17. Balsams Grand Resort, Dixville Notch. Park with permission
18. Coleman State Park, Stewartstown. Parking
19. Murphy Dam, Lake Francis. Parking. South side, too
20. Lake Francis Campground, Pittsburg. Parking
21. Second Connecticut Lake, Pittsburg. Parking at boat launch
22. Deer Mt. Campground, Pittsburg. Parking
23. U.S. Customs U.S./Canadian Border. Parking

Bodies of Water

While the White Mountains generally have higher and more dramatic summits, the North Country is full of beautiful large bodies of water dispersed between the mountains and woodlands. The North Country is more reminiscent of the Adirondacks National Forest than the White Mountains National Forest.

1. Red Pond, Mt. Eisenhower
2. Cherry Pond, Pondicherry Wildlife Preserve
3. Unknown Pond, Kilkenny unincorporated township
4. Kilburn Pond, Kilkenny
5. South Pond, Stark
6. Christine Lake, Stark. Off trail .5 mile. Trailhead
7. Lake Gloriette, Dixville Notch at Balsams Resort
8. Lake Abeniki, Dixville
9. Mud Pond, Dixville
10. Nathan Pond, Dixville
11. Little Diamond Pond, Stewartstown
12. Big Diamond Pond, Stewartstown
13. Clarksville Pond, Clarksville
14. Lake Francis, Pittsburg, Clarksville
15. First Connecticut Lake, Pittsburg
16. Eagle Pond, Pittsburg
17. Round Pond, Pittsburg
18. Second Connecticut Lake, Pittsburg
19. Third Connecticut Lake, Pittsburg
20. Moose Flowage, Pittsburg
21. Fourth Connecticut Lake, Pittsburg

Rivers

The Cohos Wilderness Trail crosses a number of major New England rivers and their tributaries. Some are placid slow moving waters, some can be fast moving and even dangerous under high water conditions.

1. Saco River, Crawford Notch
2. Ammonoosuc River, Bretton Woods
3. Johns River watershed, Jefferson. Cherry Pond area
4. Israel River, Jefferson and Lancaster
5. Upper Ammonoosuc River, Stark
6. Nash Stream, Stratford, Odell
7. Connecticut River, Pittsburg

Summits Over 4000 Feet

1. Mt. Isolation, Montalban Range. 4,005 feet
2. Mt. Eisenhower, Southern Presidentials. 4,761 feet
3. Mt. Waumbek, Pliny Range. 4,006 feet
4. Mt. Cabot, Pilot Range. 4,160 feet

Summits Over 3500 Feet

1. Mt. Davis, Montalban Range. 3,840 feet
2. Mt. Martha (Cherry Mt.), Dartmouth Range. 3,573 feet
3. Mt. Starr King, Pliny Range. 3,913 feet
4. South Weeks, Pliny Range. 3,885 feet
5. Middle Weeks, Pliny Range. 3,634 feet
6. Mt. Weeks, Pliny Range. 3,901 feet
7. Terrace, Pilot Range. 3,640 feet

8. The Bulge, Pilot Range. 3,920 feet
9. The Horn, Pilot Range. 3,905 feet
10.Mt. Sugarloaf, Northeast Peaks. 3,701 feet
11.Mt. Muise, Whitcomb Range. 3,610 feet. No trail

Summits Over 3000 Feet

1. Mt. Crawford, Montalban Range. 3,129 feet
2. Crawford Dome, Montalban Range. 3,100 feet
3. Mt. Resolution, Montalban Range. 3,428 feet. Just off trail
4. Giant Stairs, Montalban Range. 3,460 feet
5. Owlshead, Dartmouth Range. 3,258 feet
6. South Percy Peak, Nash Stream Forest. 3,220 feet
7. North Percy Peak, Nash Stream Forest. 3,418 feet
8. Baldhead South, Kelsey Notch region. 3,097 feet
9. Dixville Peak, Dixville Notch region. 3,482 feet
10.Mt. Magalloway, Pittsburg. 3,360 feet
11.Deer Mt., Pittsburg. 3,005 feet. Trail abandoned at top
12.Salmon Mt., Boundary Mts. 3,362 feet. Boundary clearing
13.Mt. D'Urban, Boundary Mts. 3,000 feet. Boundary clearing

Other Summits

1. Rogers Ledge, Kilkenny region. 2,945 feet
2. Bald Mountain, E. Nash Stream Forest. 2,380 feet. No trail
3. Victor Head, E. Nash Stream Forest. 2,165
4. Mt. Gloriette, Dixville Notch. 2,780 feet
5. Sanguinary Mt., Dixville Notch. 2,746 feet
6. Mt. Covill, Pittsburg. 2,033 feet. No formal trail

Bald or Cleared Summits, Ledges, Cliffs and Outlooks

1. Mt. Crawford
2. Crawford Dome
3. Mt. Resolution
4. Giant Stairs (cliffs and "Downlook")
5. Mt. Davis
6. Mt. Isolation
7. Mt. Eisenhower
8. Mt. Martha
9. Owlshead
10. Mt. Starr King
11. Mt. Weeks (from trail)
12. Terrace Mt.
13. Bunnell Rock
14. Mt. Cabot
15. The Horn
16. Rogers Ledge
17. Victor Head
18. South Percy

19. North Percy
20. Sugarloaf Arm
21. Mt. Sugarloaf
22. Headwaters meadows
23. Gadwah Notch
24. Baldhead South
25. Kelsey Notch
26. Dixville Peak
27. Mt. Gloriette
28. Table Rock
29. Second Brother (Third Cliff)
30. Mt. Sanguinary
31. Tumble Dick Notch
32. Stewartstown highlands
33. Mt. Covill
34. Deer Mt.
35. Boundary clearings

Other Fine Viewpoints

1. Suspension Bridge, Saco River, Frankenstein Cliffs, Crawfords
2. Route 302 in notch. View of walls of Crawford Notch
3. Mt. Washington Hotel. Sweeping view of Presidential Range
4. Pondicherry Reserve. Magnificent view Presidentials,Wildlife
5. Route 115 in Jefferson. Broad vista of Pilot and Pliny Ranges
6. Route 115A, Jefferson. Beautiful view Presidentials, Pliny Range
7. Owlshead Trailhead. Views of Jefferson Meadows, Pliny,Pilots
8. Unknown Pond. Magnificent view of The Horn.
9. Bell Hill Bridge. Views of Upper Ammonoosuc River Valley
10. Christine Lake. Views of Victor Head, Percy Peaks, Long Mt.
11. West Side Rd. Views of remote forests and peaks
12. Nash Stream Headwaters. Views of remote peaks south/west
13. Muise Bowl. Fine mountain bowl with high meadows
14. Gadwah Notch. Great vista of remote Northeast Peaks
15. Dixville Notch from road. Spectacular cliffs and spires
16. Balsams Hotel. Beautiful grounds of fine hotel
17. Diamond Ponds Rd. Sweeping views of rarely seen country
18. Creampoke Rd., Fine vista of Connecticut River valley
19. Ben Young Hill. Good views north into Canada and south
20. Lake Francis Dam. Views of great lake, vast forested country
21. Lake Francis State Park. Views from lake. Wildlife viewing
22. US Gen. picnic grounds. Vast lake offers sweeping views of peaks
23. Ramblewood Road. Views across First Lake to remote peaks
24. Second Lake boat launch. This water gem unveils peaks in Maine
25. Moose Flowage. Backwater bogs and boundary mountains
26. Third Lake. Views across lonesome lake and low peaks

Unique Geological Features

Natural Wonders

1. Crawford Notch-glacier hewn U-shaped valley
2. Jefferson Dome, Jefferson. Flat valley was once the bottom of huge glacial Lake Hitchcock
3. Devil's Hopyard, Stark. Ice gulch
4. Devil's Jacuzzi. Natural "jacuzzi" in Nash Stream
5. Dixville Notch. Extremely narrow rugged notch with rock spires
6. Flume Brook. Small flume being carved out of solid rock by Flume Brook

Water Enroute

Much of The Cohos Trail is blessed with ample water. However, there are sections where very little water is available. Lack of water can be expected above 3,000 feet in most places—high Presidentials, Montalban and Cherry Mountain ridges, much of the Kilkenny Ridge Trail, Percy Peaks, Gadwah Notch to Baldhead South and Kelsey Notch. Dixville Peak to Dixville Notch.

Be sure to carry at least 48 ounces of fresh water with you at all times. Fill bottles and canteens at any clear, fast running stream or spring to ensure you will have enough water for a long trip to lower ground and a steady source of water. (Treat the water to be safe from *Giardia* and other intestinal bugs.)

Excellent, well known springs can be found high on the southwest side of Starr King, and high on the southeast side of Sugarloaf (old well).

Reliable Water
1. Dry River, Montalban Range
2. Ammonoosuc River. Must be treated

3. Mt. Starr King spring, Mt. Starr King. Pliny Range
4. Bunnell Notch. Between Mt. Weeks and Mt. Terrace
5. Willard Notch. Between Terrace and Mt. Cabot
6. Cold Stream, Kilkenny forests
7. South Pond. Developed water supply
8. Rowells Brook, Eastern Nash Stream Forest
9. Long Mt. Brook off Percy Loop. Nash Stream Forest
10. Nash Stream, Nash Stream Forest
11. Sugarloaf Mt. Well, Sugarloaf Mt. 1,000 feet below summit
11. Nash Stream Headwaters, Northern Nash Stream Forest
12. Branch of Phillips Brook, Kelsey Notch (treat in mid summer)
13. Cascade Brook, Dixville Notch
14. Flume Brook, Dixville Notch
15. Mud Pond canal. Chain of ponds country. Dixville
16. Coleman State Park. Developed water supply
17. Labrador Brook Off Cedar Stream Rd. Pittsburg
18. Lake Francis Campground Developed water supply
19. Deer Mt. Campground. Developed water supply

Human-Made Features

World Class Hotels
1. Mount Washington, Bretton Woods
2. The Balsams, Dixville Notch

Supplies or Food Enroute
1. Crawford Notch area: Twin Mountain, Bartlett
2. Mount Washington Hotel gift shop
3. Bretton Woods shops
4. Jefferson village general stores
5. Stark village general store
6. Balsams Hotel gift shop
7. Pittsburg village stores
8. Lake Francis and First Lake area stores and campgrounds

Nearest Camping—Public
1. Dry River Camp. Rte 302, 1 mi. N. of Davis Path
2. Zealand Camp. Rte. 302, Twin Mt. Just off highway
3. Sugarloaf Camp. Rte. 302, Twin Mt. Half mile S. of Rte. 3
4. Milan Hill State Park Rte. 110A, Milan. 5 miles from South Pond
6. Coleman State Park Diamond Ponds Rd., Stewartstown
7. Lake Francis Camp. River Rd., Pittsburg
8. Deer Mountain Camp. Route 3, Pittsburg

Nearest Camping, Private

1. Crawford Notch Campground, Rte. 302, 1 mi. north of Notchland
2. Mt. Deception Campground, Cherry Mt. Road & Rte. 302. Bretton Woods
3. Isreal River Campground, half mile east of Route 115A. Jefferson
4. Lantern Campground, half mile west of Starr King trail. Jefferson
5. Log Haven Campground, four miles east of Dixville Notch. Millsfield
6. Hidden Acres Campground, Rte. 3, Lake Francis. Pittsburg
7. Mountain View Campground, Rte. 3, First Lake inlet. Pittsburg
8. Ramblewood Campground, Rte. 3, First Lake inlet. Pittsburg

Other Private Camping
1. Roger's Camp, Rte. 2. Lancaster
2. Jefferson Camp, Rte. 2. Jefferson
3. Big Rock Camp, Rte. 3. Stratford
4. Maplewoods Camp, Rte. 26. Colebrook

Hospitals
1. Littleton, Littleton, NH
2. Weeks Memorial, Lancaster, NH
3. Androscoggin Valley, Berlin, NH
4. Upper Connecticut Valley, Colebrook, NH

Roads and Railbeds Used as Trail

Only a handful of miles are spent on developed roads and along railroad rights of way, making the CT a rarely interrupted woodlands experience.

1. Route 302. Bretton Woods. Major highway. 1 mile
2. NH Route 115. Jefferson. 1.3 miles
3. NH Route 115A. Jefferson. 2.5 miles
4. Old B&M railbed. Jefferson and Whitefield. Abandoned rail line
5. NH Route 110. Stark, just north of South Pond. Road crossing
6. Percy Road. Stark. Paved town road. Half mile.
7. Nash Stream Road. Dirt forest road. Stratford and Odell. 1.9 miles
8. Route 26. Dixville Notch. Road crossing
9. Diamond Ponds Road. Stewartstown. Gravel road
10. Heath Road. Stewartstown. Narrow wooded lane. 2 miles
11. Bear Rock Road. Stewartstown. Paved farm road. 1.8 miles
12. Haines Hill Road. Stewartstown. Degraded, four-wheeler track. Over 2 miles
13. Creampoke Road. Stewartstown. Dirt road junction.
14. East Road/Covill Road. Stewartstown. Short dogleg in forest. Half mile
15. Old Ferguson Road. Stewartstown and Clarksville. Abandoned lane. 1.2 miles
16. Clarksville Pond Road. Clarksville. Farm lane. Half mile.
17. Route 145, Creampoke and Old County Roads (until trails are complete). Clarksville. 5 miles
18. Crawford Road. Pittsburg. Dirt lane. 3/4 mile.
19. Cedar Stream Road. Pittsburg. Good gravel tote road. 6 miles
20. Route 3. Pittsburg. More than 16 miles in 1999 and 2000. Fewer than 3 miles when trails are complete.

Be Prepared:
Carry the Basics

Camping Gear

The difference between a successful hike and a miserable one is equipment. Chose your equipment well and keep it as light weight as humanly possible.

1. Light-weight tent and rain fly
2. Aluminum frame pack
3. Sleeping bag rated for the season
4. Sleeping foam roll
5. Flashlight or hikers candle
6. Primus stove
7. Swiss Army knife
8. Roll of cord or wire
9. Water filter kit or treatment tablets
10. Several quart bottles for water
11. Waterproof match bottle
12. Pot or pan
12. Aluminum foil and ziplock bags
13. Garbage bags
14. Duct tape

Clothing and Shoes

I have seen so many people enter the mountains with T-shirts, shorts and sneakers and a day pack full of soda and chips that I am surprised more people do not disappear for good in the mountain folds of Coos County. Then there are the folks with high-heeled shoes on a trail, or families with tiny children hiking too many miles without water or supplies of any kind.

Do yourself a favor and stay out of the forests unless you have the basics spelled out below. You may not need a parka in July, but you might find yourself praying for one in early June or in early September.

1. Plastic rain poncho
2. Knit wool cap
3. Several changes of socks
4. Sweater or two
5. Windbreaker or parka
6. Gloves or mittens
7. Non-cotton pants
8. Sweat bandana
9. Waterproof, low-impact hiking boots
10. Broad-brim hat in fly season

Food and Drink

Long distance hikers can consume ungodly amounts of food in a day, usually twice the calories they are accustomed to eating. Bring plenty of food and a powdered beverage mix to break up the monotony of drinking water morning, noon and night.

1. Lots of gorp
2. Fresh fruit: apples and oranges keep well
3. Dried fruit
4. Jerky
5. Chocolate
6. Pasta or rice dishes
7. Canned meat, poultry, or fish
8. Freeze dried entrees
9. Fresh carrots and peppers
10. Potatoes for roasting or boiling
11. Ice tea or lemonade mix
12. Tea or coffee
13. Dried milk
14. Biscuit/pancake mix
15. Salt

First Aid

Purchase a good hiker's first aid kit or at least carry the following items with you:

1. Ace bandage
2. Band-aids and adhesive pads
3. Mole skin for blisters
4. Aspirin or other pain relievers
5. Antiseptic cream
6. Salt tablets

Comforts

The greatest luxury on the trail is to heat water, dip a face cloth in the steaming hot liquid, and sink your face into it. Heaven. The second greatest luxury is an ample supply of toilet paper. Be sure to take:

1. Toilet paper
2. Feminine sanitary goods
3. Face cloth
4. Toothbrush and paste
5. Deodorant
6. Bug repellent

In Case of Emergency

Self Rescue

The greatest danger of all on The Cohos Trail is hypothermia. More people perish or have to be rescued because they get so chilled that they cannot fend for themselves, and in a hundred cases over the last century, die in the mountains.

Avoid getting wet at all costs. Wet clothing is the talisman of doom.

If you are disoriented because of hypothermia, you haven't got a chance. If you are hypothermic, you can't rescue yourself.

The second most troublesome problem is a leg or ankle fracture. If you are hiking alone, this injury can jeopardize your life. In many areas on the CT, you are many miles from a road let alone a residence, so you will have to perform a self rescue.

Depending on the severity of the fracture, you have various options. The best one, which allows some mobility, is to cut two stout sticks and place each on either side of the leg. Now get out that roll of duct tape that you should carry with you all the time in the wilds. With the sticks projecting just a half inch below the bottom of your shoe (to help take the weight), wrap the duct tape around the sticks and your leg four or five times and at intervals a few inches apart, all the way from the ankle to the knee, or to the crotch if necessary. Cut a long stick to lean on and help you balance. Now walk out the best that you can, choosing the shortest possible route.

Falls also injure and kill people in mountains of Coos County. Stay off steep terrain if the rocks and soils are wet or covered with moss or algae. Most falls that injure hikers (not climbers) are due to slipping on slippery surfaces.

Cuts or puncture wounds from tools can present a serious problem if the wound lances a vein or artery. Should that hazard befall you, make a tourniquet from a belt, cord, or duct tape. (Great stuff, duct tape!)

There are a thousand other ways to get into trouble in the backcountry, but the odds of doing so are so remote that there is no need to bother wasting ink and paper.

Be sure you have the basics for emergencies:
1. Ace bandage
2. Duct tape
3. Good sharp knife
4. Wool cap
5. Rain poncho
6. Whistle
7. Flashlight or hikers candle lantern
8. Bandages
9. Matches

INDEX

Y

Z

Want Maps of The Cohos Trail?

Set of seven maps (front and back on two easy-to-handle pages), provide the details for a safer, more interesting trek. Includes the White Mountains, Jefferson Dome, the Kilkenny wilds, Nash Stream Forest, Dixville Notch country, and the Connecticut Lakes region (both south and north).

Important features are highlighted with graphic bullets. So at a glance you'll know where the tallest peaks and cliffs are, where to stay and get supplies, what views are available, when to tank up with water, and so much more.

Protected in a big plastic zip-lock bag, The Cohos Trail maps will enhance your wilderness journey.

Maps $10, shipping, $2 first set. $1. each addl. set. Order on page 237.

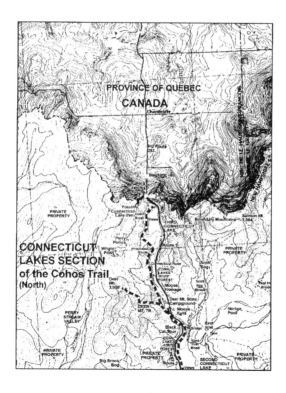

Other Great Books by Nicolin Fields Publishing, Inc.

You can find these books at your local book store, or send this order form (please photocopy), or all 800-431-1579.

The Cohos Trail The Guidebook to NH's Great Unknown
by Kim Robert Nilsen

Hikers from all over are discovering the newly developed Cohos Trail which covers 160 miles of NH's far-northern Coos County, where moose reign and only loons break the grand mountain silence. 240 pages. Index. Photos. Maps. $17.95

Maps of Cohos Trail   (See page 235.)

Bicycle Across America by Barbara Siegert

A guide to five classic cross-country adventures. Includes preparation tips, maps, and tour notes. Dare to go the distance! 208 pages. $14.95

Mountain Biking New Hampshire's State Parks and Forests
by Linda Chestney

NH boasts 164,000 acres of state parks, forests, nature areas, and reservoirs—a mecca for mountain bike adventures. These trails rides deliver just what you expect from New Hampshire—beautiful wilderness and classic New England scenery. Route notes and maps. 176 pages. $14.95

Medicinal Herbal Therapy A Pharmacist's Viewpoint
by Steven Ottariano, R.Ph.

New choices in drug-free remedies—natural healing from medicinal herbs. Registered pharmacist, Steve Ottariano, offers a balanced perspective on traditional Western medicine and complementary treatments. 192 pages. Index. Appendixes. $14.95

A Little Kinder Than Necessary A Collection of Character-Building Secrets by Beth Taber

"Words of wisdom, gathered into a delightful bouquet, bunched with charming illustrations... you'll find that the pages of this book please the eyes and challenge the soul. I enjoyed every one." Kaye Cook, Ph.D., psychologist, professor, author, mother of two. 96 pages, 6" x 6" $9.95

Bicycling Southern NH by Linda Chestney

Newly revised and expanded second edition of this popular book with maps, route notes, and attractions along the route. A great way to shape up with exercise while experiencing the beauty of New Hampshire's backroads and byways. 48 routes. 224 pages. 2000 edition. $17.95

Order Form
(Please photocopy)

Name_____

Address_____

City_____

Phone_____

Email_____

Send check or money order to:
Nicolin Fields Publishing, Inc.
3 Red Fox Road
North Hampton, NH 03862

Credit card orders, please call: 800 431-1579

Books
__Bicycle Across America, $14.95   _____

__Mountain Biking NH State Parks, $14.95   _____

__Medicinal Herbal Therapy, $14.95   _____

__A Little Kinder Than Necessary, $9.95   _____

__The Cohos Trail, $17.95   _____

__Bicycling Southern NH, $17.95   _____

Shipping, $4 first book, $1. each addl.   _____

Maps
__Cohos Trail Maps, $10.   _____

__Shipping, $2. first set of maps, $1. each addl.   _____

Total enclosed: _____

Questions? Call 603 964-1727

**Kim Robert Nilsen and granddaughter,
Sage Elizabeth, in Stewartstown, NH.**

About the Author...

Kim Robert Nilsen grew up in the '50s, playing in the woods, ponds, and streams of what remained of the farms in northern Westchester County, New York. He never lost his love for the forests, so when he moved his young family to northern New Hampshire in the early 1970s, he bought a compass and simply took off to explore the Granite State's most remote territory, Coos County, north of the White Mountains.

Today, Kim lives with his wife, Catherine, in Spofford, NH on a small hardscrabble farm with eight miniature Australian shepherd dogs, three tiny horses, two goldfish, and two geriatric sheep. The kids have grown and moved away.

From a little breezeway office, he writes books and manages a small non-profit association that builds and cares for The Cohos Trail.

An avid outdoorsman, the author has climbed, hiked, and skied throughout the mountains and deserts out west, all over New England, and the Adirondacks. But he is most fond of the isolated and unknown regions of New Hampshire's far north. When he first moved to New Hampshire, he took a job as a newspaper reporter (and later wrote for *Yankee* magazine) and was able to scour Coos County. He'd see back country in his forays around the region and on the weekends he would return to bushwhack in the wilds.

In 1978, he had tramped so much of the remote reaches of Coos that an idea evolved to build a long-distance trail over the central elevated spine of the county. He wrote an editorial about it in the *Coos County Democrat* newspaper but not a soul responded. That changed in 1996 when 55 people came to a public meeting about the concept, and The Cohos Trail Association was born.